Advance praise for
Millionaire Down the Road

"When it comes to tax planning, I've seen a lot of people who talk the talk—but don't walk the walk. This story is different. Rankin Hodgins is the real deal when it comes to aggressive tax planning. His strategy isn't for everyone, but it's worked exceptionally well for him over a long period of time."

—Grant Block
Chartered Accountant, CPA (NV)
Vancouver, B.C.

"I've had the pleasure of meeting Rankin Hodgins on a number of occasions. What jumps out at me is how well he has managed to balance risk and reward. As a former professional football player and now a coach, I need to balance risk against potential reward on every call I make. To do this successfully over thirty-five years in the investment arena—now that's a real achievement!"

—Dave Dickenson
Offensive coordinator
Calgary Stampeders, CFL

"A good investment story is like fine wine—hard to find and better with age. This is a good one. As the owner/winemaker of a boutique winery, I know that Mother Nature doesn't always deliver on time or as promised. Rankin's investment philosophy grew out of a life philosophy forged on the family farm in Depression-era Saskatchewan. This well-grounded story has it all—investment wisdom, an actual thirty-five-year investment history and a fascinating life story. Add a great glass of wine and you're in for a fine read."

—David Enns
Laughing Stock Vineyards
Penticton, B.C.

"Not only a risk-and-return story, *Millionaire Down the Road* is also a father-and-son story that captures the work ethic and lessons learned from the Great Depression of the 1930s to the great recession of 2008. The hard-earned wisdom of being Prairie born, raised and tempered resonates throughout the book. My advice to you is simple—put this one on your 'to read' list!"

—Don Proteau
Certified Financial Planner
Vancouver, B.C.

"My business is football, and my results are measured every time I step on the field. It's no different off the field, so when I see a thirty-five-year track record of consistent investment success, I know that someone has done something very special. Now that I play for the Riders, I can understand why Mr. Hodgins feels so strongly about his Saskatchewan roots. You don't get this feeling anywhere else in the world!"

—Geroy Simon
Professional athlete
Saskatchewan Roughriders, CFL

MILLIONAIRE
DOWN THE ROAD
Secrets of the ultimate tax-efficient investor

Douglas R. Hodgins
Foreword by Kenneth Corba

Millionaire Down the Road Media Inc.
www.millionairedowntheroad.com

Layout and design: Nathan Waddington, typographic.ca
Cover photo: Michelle Ramberg of Roth and Ramberg Photography Inc. Used with permission.
Cover design: Nathan Waddington and Yvonne Ren
Author photo: Rob Hebden Photography
Writing: Joshua Hergesheimer
Editing: Naomi Pauls, Paper Trail Publishing

LIBRARY AND ARCHIVES CANADA CATALOGUING IN PUBLICATION

Hodgins, Douglas R., author
        Millionaire down the road : secrets of the ultimate tax-efficient investor / Douglas R. Hodgins.

ISBN 978-0-9920322-0-3 (pbk.)

        1. Hodgins, Rankin. 2. Businessmen—Canada—Biography.
3. Investments—Canada. 4. Finance, Personal—Canada. I. Title.

HC112.5.H64H64 2013   338.092   C2013-905352-2

Typeset in Garamond Premier Pro and Cronos Pro on 60 lb. #2 Husky FSC offset paper

Printed in Canada by Friesens

To the memory of my mother

Daphne Rosabella Louise (Dundas) Hodgins

Who taught me to stand up for what's right,
Encouraged me to chase my dreams
And be the best I could possibly be.

Disclaimer

Contents

List of Figures / xi
Foreword *by Kenneth Corba* / xiii

Introduction / 1
1 March 9, 2009 / 7
2 Pitching the Book to Dad / 15
3 Early Life on the Farm / 19
4 Education & the Granary / 27
5 Family & Working Life / 37
6 Save Your Money / 43
7 The Magic of Compound Interest / 53
8 Leveraged Investing: Know All the Facts / 61
9 Understanding Investment Risk / 75
10 It's Your Money: Don't Give It Away Without a Fight / 91
11 Dad's Thirty-Five-Year Investment Journey / 105
12 The Numbers Tell the Story / 123
13 It's Not What You Earn, It's What You Keep / 147
14 Was It All Worthwhile? / 155
15 Lessons Learned From My Dad / 159

Acknowledgements / 185
About the Author / 189
Index / 190

Figures

1 Dad's investment history, 1978–2012 / 124
2 Gross investment portfolio & debt outstanding, 1978–2012 / 126
3 Net investment portfolio growth, 1978–2012 / 127
4 One-year investment returns, 1978–2012 (%) / 129
5 Five-year compound investment returns, 1983–2012 (%) / 130
6 Ten-year compound investment returns, 1987–2012 (%) / 131
7 Sources of capital, 1978 & 2012 / 135
8 Total debt outstanding, 1978–2012 / 140
9 Average margin ratios, 1981–2012 (%) / 141
10 Margin ratios, 1978–2012 (%) / 143
11 Net cash flow & income taxes paid, 2007–2012 (in $) / 149
12 Big Three bank holdings: Capital gains analysis / 151
13 Margin ratios & five-year compound returns, 1987–2011 / 156

Foreword

I T WAS DURING OCTOBER 2003 ON A CRISP, CLEAR EARLY AFTERNOON IN BUENOS AIRES. Doug Hodgins and I were sitting in an outdoor café called La Biela. Unusual for me in my adult life, I had nothing I needed to do that afternoon and nowhere I needed to be. We were simply enjoying a rich cup of coffee and the sights and sounds of the bustling Recoleta district.

At some point, as we became a bit philosophical, Doug turned to me and said, "Have I ever told you about my father's investment story?" By this time I had come to know Doug, a Canadian financial advisor, pretty well over a period of several years. We had met at an investment conference and soon hit it off as friends. We had clients in common and shared a passion for golf and travel.

However, Doug had never really said anything remarkable to me about his father. For some reason I expressed an interest that day, and he began to tell me a fascinating and compelling story about his father's approach to investing and the long-term success he had achieved after starting with only a modest amount of money.

Rankin Hodgins never earned more than $65,000 per year in his working career and started his investment portfolio in 1978 with $200,000. Twenty-five years later, his net worth had grown to over $4.5 million without adding any additional investment capital. It wasn't so much the fact that he compounded money at an attractive rate over time; it was how he did it that intrigued me.

At that time I was the New York–based CEO and chief investment officer of Pimco Equity Advisors. I managed a $2-billion mutual fund and supervised a team of portfolio managers investing over $14 billion in assets. My investment perspective came from an MBA at the University of Michigan, a CFA and twenty years' experience as a professional money manager.

As Doug told me about his father that afternoon, there was something so charming and authentic about his story that captured my imagination, and I began to look at a lifetime of investing in a different way. I was sufficiently inspired by this story that within the next year I made a trip to visit Mr. Hodgins, who lived in Lethbridge, Alberta, about as far away from Wall Street as one can get. He turned out to be one of the most memorable characters I have met during a long career in the investment business.

Eventually I started my own investment fund, which I continue to manage today using many of the same principles outlined in this book. *Millionaire Down the Road* chronicles the life and investment journey of Rankin Hodgins. His philosophy and common sense views on money and investing reflect an eternal wisdom developed over a lifetime on the prairies of Canada. I'm sure you'll find the story of this authentic, self-made man as inspirational as I did. It may even alter your view of investing.

—Kenneth Corba
New York, New York

Introduction

THE WAY MY DAD REMEMBERS, IT WAS A COLD MORNING, EVEN BY THE SASKATCHEWAN STANDARDS OF HIS YOUTH. The 12th of January, 1978. Minus 33 degrees. "So cold I could barely get the car to start," he tells me. A little smile spreads across his face, as it often does when he recalls a particularly strong memory.

I shuffle through my own memories of Prairie mornings: little things—being bundled up in a thick winter coat, furiously scraping the windshield, trying not to inhale the frigid air too deeply. But it's been three decades since I've seen a full Prairie winter, and my memories of those days are all fuzzy and romantic, much like the broad strokes used by those Impressionist painters.

On that particular morning my father, Rankin Hodgins, was standing in the driveway, stamping his feet to warm them as he scraped the windshield and coaxed his car to life. He had kissed my mother, Daphne, for good luck as he headed out the door.

"Yes sir, it was a miserably cold day," Dad says. "But I had an appointment. And I wasn't going to be late for that."

Dad parked in front of the local CIBC branch in Claresholm, Alberta, with ten minutes to spare. He left his car running and cranked up the heater as he sat flipping through the pages in the folder he had brought along. One last look over the numbers, just to be sure everything adds up, he told himself.

At 9:00 a.m. sharp, the window sign flipped over. OPEN FOR BUSINESS. Dad cracked the door and got out. A frigid blast of wind hit him as he hustled inside, taking his breath away.

That meeting would change my dad's life. He went into that bank as a fifty-seven-year-old man nearing retirement. He came out with a loan for $18,000. Nothing particularly special about that, you might think. People borrow money all the time. But isn't borrowed money supposed to be for a family vacation or a home renovation? This was a loan for investment purposes.

Dad added the loan proceeds to $200,000 of his own money to begin a program of what we in the financial world call leveraged investing. Over the next three decades, this leveraged investing program would create more than $9 million of wealth, far exceeding his wildest expectations.

The way I see it, it's a good thing Dad kept that appointment.

~

My dad wasn't a financial whiz when he started investing. He wasn't a no-holds-barred risk-taker either. I tell his story to let you know that you don't have to be a genius or a gambler to be successful in the world of investing. What Dad did have—the most important characteristic any investor can have—was the right outlook.

Dad grew up on a farm in Saskatchewan in the 1930s, during the depths of the Great Depression. He watched his parents struggle to put food on the table, but never once did he hear them complain. The way Dad sees it, his folks knew enough about farming to know there are some things in life you can't control, no matter how hard you try. The only thing you *can* control is how you respond.

Farmers face many variables that determine the bounty of the harvest. Will the warm spring rains arrive in time to nurture the first soft shoots? Will August bring the long hot days that mature a crop, turning swaths of summer green into fields of autumn gold? Or will an early frost wipe out everything you've worked so hard to create?

In the "Dirty Thirties," Prairie farmers watched helplessly as their fields turned to dustbowls, the shifting winds blowing their fragile soil skyward . . . and, along with it, their hopes and dreams for the future. Dad says that living through those times taught him the most important lesson of his whole life: when times are tough, don't give up. Be patient. Keep on getting things done . . . and always hope next year will be better. I tend to think the same way.

You may question wisdom like this from a guy who wears a suit and works in an office, but there are a lot of similarities between farming and investing. Just like farmers, good investors realize they can't control all the variables that determine whether they end up in the red or in the black. You can do your "due diligence," but wild market fluctuations can come out of nowhere, defying all logic. Companies once deemed solid, steady and well-positioned can be hammered by unrelated events half a world away. Instead of giving in to panic and fear, skilled investors have learned that the best way to respond to market turmoil is to stay calm and collected—and stick to their original investment principles.

Dad has been through a lot over the years. In 1978, when he started investing, a 6% interest rate was pretty standard. But four years later, rates had skyrocketed to 22%. How many of us could handle that? In 1987, Dad lost 20% of his gross portfolio overnight when the market crashed. In 2001, Dad lost $750,000 during the turmoil that followed the terrorist attacks of September 11. And in 2008 and early 2009, he lost more than $6 million during the banking meltdown and subsequent global economic crisis. Dad has been tested by every type of market condition that exists in the investment world.

What got him through the tough times wasn't necessarily his financial aptitude. It was his investment attitude. Each time he faced a market in free fall, he drew on those life skills he'd learned as a young boy on the family farm during the Great Depression: patience, persistence and discipline. And you know what? This outlook has worked for him, each and every time.

I believe a lot of people can benefit from hearing my dad's story. Regular people. People who don't have a financial or investing background. People with average incomes who might not read the *Financial Post* or the *Globe and Mail*, who might be frightened by the thought of putting their hard-earned money at risk—money they've carefully saved over the years.

If this sounds like you, then you'll want to read on. After all, when it comes right down to it, my father is just like thousands of other people right across this country. He believes in the value of hard work and in getting value for a dollar. At the age of ninety-one, he still gets up every day at 6:00 a.m. and spends his day reading and keeping active. The things that motivate him—becoming better at whatever he does, making sure he always has enough for a rainy day, showing concern for his family and his friends—are probably the same things that motivate you.

Of course, any financial book written by a son about his father will do more than just crunch the numbers. You'll find plenty of other investment books out there already, filled with cheerful charts and graphs illustrating the power of percentages and compound interest. This isn't a book about abstract financial concepts or a spreadsheet analysis of the market behaviour of a successful investor. This is a story written by a son about his father: a modest, dignified and determined man, a real Canadian Prairie boy who made real decisions that had real outcomes, both positive and negative, for both himself and his family.

Watching my dad manage his portfolio over the decades has taught me a lot about risks and rewards. The relationship between these two basic concepts is something every investor—whether seasoned or just starting out—should know about and understand. But most importantly, I've learned invaluable investment lessons from my dad—lessons I've used to help my clients achieve their retirement dreams. Whether or not you share his investment philosophy, I think you'll want to know how he's achieved his success. Hopefully you'll pick up a few ideas that are useful for you. Sound good? Then let's get started.

Chapter 1

March 9, 2009

I T'S EARLY IN THE MORNING WHEN THE PHONE RINGS. 6:12 a.m. to be precise. It may seem strange that I remember the exact time, but I know because I glanced at the clock radio sitting on my night table before I answered the phone, wondering who would be calling at this hour. I shouldn't have been surprised.

"Douglas," he asks when I pick up, "what should I do?"

I don't have to ask what that question means. "Dad," I begin to answer, but before I can say anything, he interrupts me. "Were you able to get through to Corba this morning?" he asks, his voice tense. "Dad, it's six o'clock in the morning. I was sound asleep till a minute ago," I reply somewhat curtly.

Ken Corba had just recently retired as the CEO and chief investment officer of Pimco Equity Advisors in New York, a firm that managed $14 billion of equity funds. He was also a family friend whom Dad had turned to for advice in the past.

"What does he have to say?" Dad asks. "And what about all those other 'bright boys' in New York he keeps in touch with? What have they got to say about the markets?"

It's March 9, 2009. The markets are tanking over the last few days. What had begun the year before with the bankruptcy of Lehman Brothers has now morphed into a crash course in disaster management. Each morning we are awaking to news of a new low as the bottom keeps dropping out of the market.

"Have you spoken to John?" I ask, rubbing the sleep from my eyes. My brother John has been my tag-team partner for the past few months, helping to keep Dad informed about the hourly changes often taking place in the market.

"He won't answer his phone," Dad snorts. "He's probably in the shower," I reply. "Not likely," Dad responds, rather tersely, but he backs off when I gently remind him about the time of day in Vancouver and the frequency of his early-morning calls. "I guess I may be coming across a little harsh," Dad concedes. "But I'm worried sick. What would *you* do, Douglas?"

I tilt my head to hold the phone on my shoulder while I reach for my robe. Better put the kettle on and get some tea happening, I say to myself. No way this is going to be a short one.

Many financial analysts had concluded that the markets were hitting the bottom in September of 2008. But then October was worse. There had been a slight uptick in December and the first few days of 2009, just enough to raise hopes and give the pundits some new material to work with. It was just a rough patch that was clearing up, they chimed in. It'll work itself out, they all agreed.

Then another drop—a big one this time. March was coming in like a lion when everyone was hoping for a lamb. The graphs popping up on computer screens were jagged red lines heading in a southerly direction, taking people's portfolios with them. Could this be the capitulation that sends even the crustiest market veterans scurrying to the sidelines, wiping out the financial future of an entire generation? Were we heading for a 1930s-style depression?

I've always found it easy to talk straight to my father. He is a practical guy who never wastes any time getting to the heart of the matter. So I knew the time for small talk had long passed. I just had to speak my mind. Trouble was, I didn't really know what to say. Even though I had spent my whole career helping clients develop and implement wealth accumulation strategies, I didn't know what to make of the current situation. We were in uncharted waters. Everything that had seemed rock-solid before now seemed to be built on sand and at risk of being swept away by the outgoing tide.

The whistling kettle interrupts my thoughts. I carefully pour the hot water as I listen to Dad's voice on the other end of the line. I can almost see him, sitting in the basement office of his Lethbridge bungalow, his "nerve centre," as the family likes to call it. Dad spends most of his days in there, reading and researching, always trying to get an edge on the markets. He has the room set up in such a way that he can see the television without having to look away from the computer screen. Right now he's probably leafing through that tattered pad of green accounting paper he's used for thirty years to track the weekly value of his portfolio, desperately looking for clues on how we got to this point. He's probably asking himself the same questions everyone in the business is asking: What the heck is going on? Why didn't I see it coming? What now?

Over the years Dad and I have often joked that maybe he should just cash everything in and "put his feet up"—you know, really retire. But there was none of that loose talk now. This was dead serious. If we didn't do something quickly to save his portfolio, the retirement he had worked so hard for would be in jeopardy. But what to do? Sell off what we could to avoid a margin call? Stay the course and risk the bank appropriating his long-held stocks and liquidating them to pay the debt—a debt that was eating up his equity by the hour?

"Douglas?" I can hear the gravity of the situation in Dad's voice. "Are you still there?"

I want to give assurances: everything will be alright, Dad. We've been through tough times before. We'll get through this. Except I can't, probably because I don't know if I believe it myself. To be honest, I'm not sure he will get through it.

Still silence. I have to come up with something. "Dad?" I say. "Remember Black Monday?" Now it's my turn to hear silence on the line. Dad is busy running through his memories of that time. Finally he answers in a quiet voice, "You think it might be that bad?"

On October 19, 1987, Dad lost a lot of money. He wasn't the only one. Investors had ridden the wave of a surging US economy that led world stock markets to new highs by the mid-'80s. The only direction anyone in the business was talking about was up, up and up.

But as Dad always likes to say, "That which can go up can also come down." He doesn't say "must always come down," like a science teacher explaining the law of gravity, because the markets don't follow laws. (If they did, investing would be like shooting fish in a barrel.) But it's clear Dad has the same amount of respect for the financial markets as a science professor has for the laws of physics.

"I remember that day in October well," Dad says. "In those days I listened to the radio to get my market updates." I always wonder what it must have been like to sit by the radio, trying hard not to pace grooves in the floor as the news reports came crackling through on the CBC. It's hard to imagine those pre-Internet days without real-time analysis from multiple sources, but back then, that was what they had. All they could do was wait with bated breath, hoping and praying for the best but expecting the worst.

"Stock-market programming on TV was minimal at that time," Dad tells me, "but I knew from the news flashes on radio and TV that things were bad. Every time I looked or listened, the numbers got worse. At the end of the day, my gross portfolio had gone from about $1.5 to around $1.2 million."

I do some quick math. "You lost $300,000 in a single day?" I exclaim, not bothering to hide the surprise in my voice. I had forgotten the number was that big. "That's right," Dad answers. "Not exactly the start to retirement I was hoping for."

That would have been stressful enough for anyone to deal with. But, true to form, Dad wasn't as worried about himself as he was about the clients whom he had advised to go into the market. Although Dad was technically retired, he had kept a desk at his old insurance agency, selling investments to a small group of friends, relatives and former clients. Nothing big, just a few GICs and some of the better-known mutual funds of the day: Templeton, Trimark and Mackenzie, to name a few.

Only a few weeks earlier, Dad had sold $15,000 worth of Templeton Growth Fund to the widowed wife of a family friend. Now he was worried sick about what she would say. "She called me at eleven o'clock that night, very distraught," Dad recalls. "I remember her saying, 'Rankin, what have you done to us?' That topped off a very difficult day."

I get the sense Dad wants to keep talking, so I stay silent. He starts in again. "I had sold my brother Ken $12,000 in Templeton funds about a week earlier. I had also sold a retired pilot $20,000 in Templeton just a few days before the crash. I said to myself, how am I going to face these people?"

Stories like these remind me what a small-town guy Dad really is. There he was, just having lost more than a third of a million dollars, and what was he worried about? The good folks of his old hometown. How would they cope? And what would they be saying (or at least thinking) about him? It's difficult to think of some big-city broker lying awake at night worrying about what his clients are thinking about him. Definitely a small-town phenomenon. Although Dad has lived in cities, he has always held fast to the belief that connection to a community relies upon everyone interacting with and caring about everyone else. Like I said, a small-town guy at heart.

~

It's 6:22 a.m. We've been on the line for ten minutes, neither of us saying much of anything, just trading silences back and forth. But out of the corner of my eye I see the numbers I'm monitoring on my television. The black lines are still dropping, but nothing like the 5% hit the markets took on the first day of the month. I know that Dad's worried sick about another market plunge that he couldn't recover from. If that were to happen, his portfolio wouldn't last long.

"Well," Dad says to me over the phone, suddenly sounding more confident. "It's 2009 and I am still here. So is my money. Somehow we'll get through this."

"But we need a strategy," I tell him. "Just watching and waiting isn't going to cut it this time." I'm unable to hide the urgency in my voice. "This isn't a crop that can just be replanted. If you don't do something soon, you'll be finished." There is a long pause on the line. "You're right, Douglas," Dad says and sighs. "So what should we do?"

"Let's go back to John's spreadsheet. I've got my copy right here. Get yours out so we can go over it." I am not quite sure why I just said this, since I know he's already got his in front of him. It's like I said it just to show that I'm in charge, that I've got it together. In reality, I'm scared.

In 1996, my brother John had done a complete analysis of Dad's investment portfolio. John crunched some numbers and found some patterns—patterns Dad didn't even know were there. That spreadsheet changed Dad's world. He was immediately sold on it, a visual printout that "laid out the truth in plain view," he always liked to say.

Dad would pore over the spreadsheet for hours. He would play the figures off against each other, comparing and contrasting complex what-if scenarios. He consulted it so frequently that the rest of the family began referring to it as Dad's bible. If we were to stand a chance of saving Dad's portfolio, the spreadsheet was the key. After careful analysis of all the key variables it showed, and even much soul searching by Dad, he decided to stay the course.

The big plunge Dad was worried about didn't happen that day, but it was anyone's guess what tomorrow would bring. After spending most of the day on the phone with my own concerned clients, I didn't even make it to bed—I fell asleep on the couch, totally exhausted.

Chapter 2

Pitching the
Book to Dad

AT THE BEGINNING I TOLD YOU THIS WAS DAD'S STORY. But Dad's story wouldn't be much good to you if it were only half told. Stories about people who have achieved financial success often play out that way: the good stuff goes in and the bad stuff gets left out. The writer makes the subject look intelligent, savvy and—most of all—justifiably wealthy. This book isn't like that.

Over the past three decades, my dad has made some good financial decisions that have made him a lot of money. He's developed strategies based on a few sound financial principles that have served him well, especially during the rough patches that are a normal part of any investment cycle. As I tell you my dad's story, I'm going to talk about some of the strategies behind his success, because I think you need to know what worked for him. But as I said before, telling you this would be only half the story.

Dad would be the first to admit that some of his investment decisions didn't play out the way he would have liked. Sometimes he just flat out made some bad decisions that got him into trouble, like when he kept buying into an apparently stable company that suddenly collapsed. Sometimes it was because Dad made decisions based on incomplete information, leaving him to mutter "If I had only known . . ." at family get-togethers for several years after. And sometimes Dad made decisions that put him into some pretty risky territory, leaving him too vulnerable to short-term market fluctuations.

So as I tell this story, it's only fair to share some of these mistakes with you. This keeps the story honest. It also keeps my dad honest and, perhaps more importantly, at least somewhat humble! Besides, not telling you about what went wrong would let a perfectly good teachable moment go by.

Dad has spent more than thirty years making decisions and living with the consequences of those decisions. He has come to some pretty strong conclusions about what he did right and what he did wrong. And he's happy to share these conclusions with you. As he himself says: "Half the battle in this game is minimizing mistakes. So if my story helps others avoid the mistakes I made, let's get it out there, because at the end of the day, we're all in this thing together."

As I said in the introduction, this book is more than just my dad's view of things. It is also my view of things. Thirty years as a professional financial planner and investment advisor have given me a financial background my dad never had. I've gone through the numbers in his portfolio from day one and observed how his investment strategy has played out. I've been able to analyze the impact of his decisions from a more objective standpoint than he ever could have. I've seen some patterns that Dad never saw, and I've drawn some of my own conclusions about his program that I will share with you. After that, you can decide if any of his strategies might work for you.

~

It was a warm evening in June 2010 when I first told Dad about my idea for this book. Initially, he wasn't impressed. "Who'd pay good money for a book about *my* investing story?" he replied. "It isn't that complicated."

"Lots of people would be interested in your story, Dad," I told him. I had rehearsed these lines on the plane ride over from Vancouver so I would be well prepared for our little discussion. I even waited until we were sitting on his back deck, in a more relaxed state, winding down as the sun settled in the western sky. "And besides, you yourself said that people could learn from your story and become better investors."

"You'll tell them the whole story?" He sounded skeptical. "The good *and* the bad?" I smiled. "I'll give them enough of each so they get the point. And I'll try my best to make you look good in the process," I said, suppressing a little chuckle.

"You will do no such thing, Douglas," he replied, laughing along. "You have to give them the straight goods so they can learn something of value. And you'll give them some advice while you're at it, right? I don't want this just to be a book about me, get it?"

"Don't worry Dad. I've got it all worked out. I think even you'll be impressed with what I've got in mind." I stopped for a moment and leaned back in my chair. I took a sip of lemonade. As I lowered the glass I spied a lone robin skillfully plucking a worm out of Dad's freshly mown lawn. Then we both fell quiet for a bit. I don't know how long. All I remember is the breeze making a whistling sound as it blew through the wicker chairs on the back deck.

"Make sure you tell them about the farm," Dad said. "You've got to include that." I nodded. "I was going to, Dad. That's the best part, after all." He went quiet again.

"You tell them my story first, you know, who I am, how I was raised, how I live my life, important things like that," he said, after thinking about it further. "And none of those fancy charts and graphs that get their heads swimming in numbers before they've even been introduced to me."

"Done, Dad, you've got it," I said. "I'll make sure that all gets in. But we have to set it up just right. You'll see."

Then we sat in silence for a long time, watching the first stars appear as the blue faded to black and night settled in. I obviously fell asleep, because when I came to Dad was no longer there. Time for bed, I said to myself somewhat contentedly. I think I've got him on board.

Chapter 3

Early Life on the Farm

MY FATHER WAS BORN ON A FARM IN NORTHERN SASKATCHEWAN. The first son of Wilfred and Rachel, Wilfred Rankin Hodgins was born on November 22, 1921. He came into the world in the small community of Wakaw, located 90 kilometres northeast of Saskatoon, just as the first fingers of winter were tightening their grip on the Prairie landscape. He was proudly named after his father Wilfred and his mother Rachel Rankin, but his parents started using his middle name early in his life and he's been known as Rankin Hodgins ever since.

My grandparents had moved to Saskatchewan three years earlier. Leaving behind the Rankin family farm in Foresters

Falls on the Ontario side of the Ottawa Valley and the Hodgins family on the Quebec side of the Ottawa Valley in Shawville, Quebec, Wilfred and Rachel moved west after their wedding in 1918. They followed the promise of prosperity, buying six quarters of farmland some 130 kilometres northeast of Saskatoon. World War 1 had just ended and people were buying again, creating an insatiable demand for a variety of agricultural products. The lure of fertile ground and tales of high agricultural prices were enough to convince Wilfred and Rachel that the western Prairies were where they wanted to start their new life together.

The farm where Dad grew up was somewhat isolated, even by today's standards. It was about 10 miles (16 km) northeast of Domremy and 16 miles (25 km) southwest of Birch Hills. My late Uncle Ken noted that while summer days could be long and glorious, the sky a crisp blue and the sun seeming to hang in the sky forever, winter was a completely different matter. "There was no traffic on the nearby road in the wintertime," he told me in one of the last telephone conversations we had prior to his passing in May 2012. "Trips to town were few and far between. The car was put up on blocks from November to April. If we wanted to go somewhere, we went by horse and cutter or by sleigh."

I remember that conversation well. Uncle Ken was near the end of a tough battle with cancer, but he became noticeably animated when I asked him about his memories of the farm. At times like this, you realize how important our connection is with the land we live on. Even though my uncle was a pharmacist, a medical doctor and had a master's degree in health administration—truly a learned man—what was important to him at the end of his life was not his learning—it was the farm.

He was weak—I could tell this by his voice—so I expected we would have a difficult but necessary discussion about life . . . You know the kind of discussion I mean: the kind where you're not quite certain what to say so you just do your best to stumble through it and hope the words come out in the spirit intended.

Once we started talking about the farm, Uncle Ken's demeanour changed completely. Although he had left the farm in Grade 9 when my grandparents moved to Prince Albert and later went on to pursue many years of education and a lifetime of work in the health profession, the farm never really left him. City folk don't get the same grounding. These were his roots, my dad's roots, our family's roots. This was where we came from. Who we were. What we stood for. This was what mattered in life and, more importantly, in my uncle's life. Thanks, Uncle Ken, for all your help, guidance and encouragement, not only with the book but with life in general.

~

I sometimes imagine what life was like in the wintertime on the farm, with snow blanketing the ground and a frigid wind blasting across frozen fields. That's a hard enough life, even in the good times. But the 1920s were not easy for farmers breaking the land to extend farming north within the province of Saskatchewan. This was heavily forested land with rich, dark soil, much different than the prairie land in the southern part of the province. The growing season was short and the threat of early fall frosts a constant concern. My dad's family was fortunate just to get by in those days. Dreams of turning a profit were nothing more than dreams. But the family was patient and kept getting things done, hoping that the next year would be better than the last.

Dad started his schooling in the rural one-room Golden Rod School in May 1929. School started in May for the first grade, as it was deemed impractical to send small children to school over the cold winter months.

"It was two and a half miles to the school, but the school was really in the middle of nowhere," Dad told me. "As soon as I could ride a horse, my father would hoist me up and off I would go. I rode bareback, and on cold days I can still remember trying to keep warm by leaning forward close to Goldie's mane."

Although it can be hard to visualize my now elderly father as a small boy, clinging tightly to the mane of his horse, when he tells the story his eyes tell me everything I need to know. "No one lived on the road I took, so it was somewhat hazardous for a young boy," he says, in the voice that fathers always use when they tell their children about the hardships they endured in the "old days." And even though I know how the story ends, I always let him finish.

"Goldie knew her way, but it was a constant struggle to hold her back on the way home. She knew that a big, juicy bag of oats would be hanging in her stall when the two of us arrived back at the farm." I love the visual Dad creates as he slowly enunciates the last line—it's almost as if I'm right there with him in the barn, watching Goldie nuzzle up to the oat bag in her stall.

In 1929, Dad's father Wilfred decided—after much deliberation—that the family farm needed to make the switch from manual to mechanical. They needed to buy some tractors. Maybe he could see into the future. Maybe it was too obvious to miss. Regardless, he sensed that the old world was changing, and old ways of doing things needed to change as well.

Grandfather moved forward swiftly, buying into the new technology in much the same manner our generation has embraced computers. However, tractors and farm machinery cost a lot more than computers, so Grandfather had to rely on the farm machinery company to extend him credit to make the change. It seemed like the right way to go at the time.

But history has a way of making seemingly good decisions look bad. The winds of change also brought a new economic reality. All the mechanization in the world couldn't bring rain.

Farmers' incomes dried up. And instead of getting better, the economy got worse. Then the effects of the Depression really began to bite. "We had enough to eat, but money was scarce," my dad always says when I ask him about those times. "Every fall a collector came from the machinery company to ask my father to at least pay off part of his account. My mother always insisted that he stay for supper, but for many years that's all he got. It took more than a decade for my parents to pay off that debt."

The years 1937 and 1938 were the worst. A particularly harsh winter was followed by a short flicker of summer. The crop yield was down, as were the prices farmers got for selling what meagre harvest they did have. Despite these mounting problems, Dad recalls that his parents were always grateful for what they had.

"We were much better off than many families in the drought-stricken southern part of the province," my dad reminisces. Dad was the eldest of the three Hodgins boys. William Arnold Hodgins, my dad's middle brother, was born in 1927, and the baby of the family, Kenneth Wallace Hodgins, was born in 1933. All three experienced the Depression from different perspectives depending on their age, but I think it had the greatest impact on my dad. "We barely survived the challenges of weather, poor crops and low prices, but Father and Mother never gave up hope and worked tenaciously to survive. Only the hardy made it through those years. We considered ourselves fortunate to be part of that group."

Dad remembers his father constantly worrying about the risk of foreclosure. In fact, the only reason the family carried on was due to the intervention of a prominent businessman in Domremy named Alfred Molstad, the legal advisor to the mortgage holders of the land, the A & E Pierce Corporation of Montreal. Instead of coming to the farm to demand payment or threaten eviction, Mr. Molstad arrived with words of encouragement. "He urged my parents not to give up on the land, to carry on, in the hope that the economy would improve."

Those hard times made a big impression on my dad. The constant scarcity of money and food stuck with him. But what he remembers most is the sense of living on a knife-edge, the thought that any day, just scraping by could turn much worse. Lessons learned from this tumultuous period left him very frugal and respectful of money. Even now, he is always on the lookout for a good deal, whether he's buying a shirt and tie or half-price pies at the market. He is living proof that "you can take the boy out of the Prairies, but you can't take the Prairies out of the boy."

Dad's perspective on money today

My dad has a healthy respect for money. But I can see how someone who just met him today might get the opposite impression, especially when he can seemingly shrug off portfolio swings of more than a million dollars a year. When I ponder Dad's remarkable ability to "stay the course" amidst such turmoil, I think this attitude has more to do with his farming roots than his financial fortitude.

On a farm, sometimes you can do all the "right" things—plow and plant on time, water well and avoid the pests—and still get the "wrong" result. Dad watched his parents do everything they could to give their crops the best chance, but you can't stop the seasons from changing ahead of schedule, and you sure can't make it rain when the sky is a cloudless blue. Lord knows there were probably sufficient prayers being offered up by penitent Prairie farmers during the '30s, but you can only do what you can do. In those circumstances, the best anyone can do is be patient, keep on getting things done . . . and hope that next year will be better.

Dad has weathered thirty-five years of market fluctuations better than a lot of people I know. What keeps him going in the rough times is his unshakeable belief that eventually things will turn out alright. His ability to "carry on" in difficult times is underpinned by his long-term perspective, determination and perhaps even his stubbornness to stay focused on achieving his goals. Of course, while there are other variables at play than just patience and persistence, we too often underestimate the importance of "just staying in the game," as my dad likes to say.

I figure Dad's ability to remain confident and stand by his investment decisions—rather than constantly tinkering with his portfolio, selling and buying frantically in response to every bump or blip in the market—is a direct outcome of his early years growing up on the farm. After all, when you think about it, what better validation is there for a belief in long-term thinking than surviving the Great Depression?

"Douglas," Dad says to me one afternoon, soon after I pitched him the idea for the book, "you might want to mention that my parents survived the worst economic crisis this part of the world has ever seen." I nod. "And you tell them I can still remember the look in my mother's eyes after seeing Father write the final cheque that paid off the farm machinery loan. I hadn't seen her that happy in a long time," he says softly.

He's never told me this before. This memory, deeply entrenched in his memory as a seventeen-year-old boy, was buried decades deep—yet instantly recalled with vivid clarity. I look over at my dad. I haven't seen him reminisce like this for ages, and it's showing on his face. His eyes light up as his mind takes him back to life growing up on the farm. I am beginning to think this book will help Dad recall a lot of old memories that haven't surfaced in a long time.

Dad continues. "I saw the land around us," Dad says, swinging his arms outward, "land that had been a dustbowl for years, now bursting with healthy crops." He smiles to himself, as if he can still feel the sun on his face and the wind in his hair. "And money that had been scarce for so many years finally started to flow again. That was a big relief. We knew we'd made it."

They had. The world didn't end, as many people had been predicting. And this young boy's realization—that nothing bad can last forever—influenced his thinking and his outlook on life. So it was inevitable that when my dad began investing at the age of fifty-seven, he would bring that same Depression-era farming mentality to managing his portfolio.

His outlook is long term, so he only owns quality companies he feels will get better over time. He has pride of ownership, only investing in businesses that he knows and can be proud of. Companies he believes in. And he is patient, looking for stable companies that pay a growing stream of dividends. In the back of his mind he always remembers life lessons learned on the farm, where sometimes doing all the right things didn't necessarily guarantee a bountiful harvest. But Dad learned enough from his "stats" classes to know that long-term probabilities will eventually play themselves out, especially given enough time.

And you know what? He's right. Dad's portfolio has grown from $200,000—his original investment in 1978—to more than $7 million today, thirty-five years later. He's actually created more than $9 million in wealth if you include the $2 million he has given to his five children over the years (yours truly included—thanks, Dad!).

Chapter 4

Education & the Granary

"D OUGLAS?" DAD CALLS OUT TO ME FROM THE KITCHEN. He's supposed to be making himself a sandwich, but it's been a while and I don't see any signs of sandwich as I enter the room. He's probably lost in his thoughts. It is happening a bit more frequently these days as I try to tease his life story out of him. I can tell he's remembered something he wants to tell me.

"Are you going to write about the granary in your book?" Dad's eyes sparkle as he savours the memory.

A granary is a small shed-like building where grain is stored in large quantities prior to being sent to market. Granaries are an important part of farm life, but in my dad's case, one played an even more important role than just storing grain.

Dad turned out to be a good student in primary school. His mother had been a teacher, so you might say he had an "extra motivation" to succeed. Like many young people in farming communities, when it came time for high school, Dad had to look farther afield. There was no secondary school in his district, and even the next district was struggling to find enough students to run a program.

"They had a community hall that would double as the high school if they could get enough pupils," Dad said. "The province of Saskatchewan provided a grant of $600 to pay the teacher's annual salary on the condition they could attract at least fifteen students. I became the fifteenth student." So on a warm September day in 1935, my father mounted his horse and rode five miles to the next district and Northern Light High School.

"It wasn't long before travelling by horseback lost a lot of its romance, especially on cold winter days," Dad reminds me (probably because he thinks Vancouver's mild climate has made me forget the bone-chilling cold of −30° Celsius). He adds, "I usually stayed at the farm home of Ole Kilden, which was close to the school, and came home for weekends."

My grandparents were motivated to see their three sons get a good education. In 1938, Dad's brother Bill also enrolled in Northern Light High School. This presented a problem for my grandfather, as he now needed to find accommodation for two sons. So my grandfather Wilfred—ever the resourceful Prairie farmer—got an idea while attending a farm auction sale. When the auctioneer was having trouble attracting bidders for a granary, my grandfather jumped in and purchased it for the princely sum of $18. Days later, Grandfather had the granary on the move, hauling it behind a team of four horses to a vacant farmyard next to the school. Problem solved.

I sometimes stop to think about my grandfather, skillfully working his team of horses, hauling that granary down the road.

I imagine him saying to himself, hopefully this will help the boys stay on track with their studies. But I also know there's a part of him that must have been thinking, great move to buy the granary. The boys will do just fine in it! In that sense my dad has inherited the practicality of his father—and in a more modern sense, so have I. Even though I've lived in Vancouver for more than thirty years, I'm immensely proud of my Saskatchewan roots. Still a Prairie boy at heart, just like my dad.

When I first began writing this book, I zeroed in on this single scene. It seemed to epitomize everything I wanted to say about life on the Prairies in those days: resourceful people making do with whatever was at hand. But as I got deeper into the story, I started to wonder. Something didn't add up in what Dad had told me. Remember that my grandfather had switched the farm over to mechanical back in 1929. So why would he still be using horses to pull the granary?

"Dad?" I call across to him. He has just sat down in his rocking chair on the back porch, and I wait until he's locked into that slow rhythm of back-and-forth before I continue.

"Dad, are you sure it was horses?" I raise my glass of lemonade and shake the ice cubes around, as if to deflect the attention from my question. Dad doesn't really like it when I probe his recollections. I think he feels slightly insulted, as if I don't trust his memory.

He looks over. "What do you mean?" The words come out slowly. A measured response, but one that sets the tone for this discussion. He feels interrogated.

"Something just doesn't add up," I say, glancing down at my notebook. I pretend to be checking my notes, but the truth is that I don't want our eyes to meet.

"Of course it was horses," Dad snaps. "I remember him hitching them up. Those horses sure snorted and bucked when they realized what it was they were going to be pulling."

"But Dad," I continue, as gingerly as possible, "the farm switched to mechanical in 1929. Why would Grandpa not just use his tractor to pull the granary?"

There is a long silence. Dad's forehead furrows. I can tell he is somewhat annoyed that I'm questioning him, but I can also see from his face that he's delving back into his memories. He won't admit it, but he's doing some verification of his own.

"You know," he starts in, "your grandfather kept that team of horses for a good number of years after he bought the tractors. They were damn fine horses. Father said it'd be a shame to sell them off, seeing as they'd been working members of the farm their whole lives. Better to let them stay and keep them busy."

I don't say anything. Instead, I just keep my head down as I flip through my notebook.

Dad goes silent too. Then he sighs. "You know, it's the darndest thing," he finally says. "I can't for the life of me actually pin it down. I remember the horses being hitched up daily, like I said, just to keep them busy. But Douglas, to be honest I can't recall whether the granary was pulled by horses or by a tractor."

I wait until it is clear he's said everything he wants to say. I can tell it bothers him, the idea that he may not be 100% certain on something so central to his upbringing. I quickly try to focus his attention elsewhere.

"Well, why don't I ask Uncle Ken?" I say. "He might know."

"Ken wouldn't know," Dad retorts. "He was just a kid at the time, five years old. Oh, he might have an opinion on the matter, always having been the family historian," he says, "but he certainly wouldn't have known for sure." As Dad says this he sits up a bit straighter, just like Uncle Ken did before he launched into one of his farm stories.

"Besides," Dad continues, "you know what? There really aren't many people left to verify these stories. So just like good wine, they get better with age." He smiles.

"No worries, Dad," I say, thankful he doesn't seem too bothered by this gap in his memory. "I think I'm going with horses in the book. It's more authentic anyway, and I like the visual it creates."

Dad looks away and shakes his head. "But really, I should know," he mutters to himself. Then he eases himself up and shuffles towards the door, glass in hand. I knew he couldn't leave it hanging like that. I call after him.

"Dad, it was more than seventy years ago," I say. "It's okay if you don't remember."

He grunts, but doesn't look back. The screen door closes softly behind him. I figure he'll be pondering that one for a while, but it doesn't matter as I love this story and it's definitely going in the book.

⁓

Autumn 1938. Dad and his brother Bill took up residence in the granary during the week so they could attend school, returning to the family farm on weekends. But as fall turned to winter and the mercury dropped, Dad and Bill ended up hosting another local boy, Virgil Gilbertson. Virgil was from the neighbouring district, and rather than risk frostbite on bitterly cold nights, he would bunk in with the boys.

As far as granaries go, Dad figures it was a fairly decent one. "Well constructed," he'd always say if anyone asked him. "Probably would've done an excellent job of storing grain," he would add. "But as far as living quarters go, it was pretty basic."

"Basic?" I reply. "No, Dad, the Super 8 motel chain is basic. A shack with one-ply lumber walls and no insulation is not basic. It was more frontier than basic."

He grins. "The walls were just thick enough to take the edge off the icy prairie winds, but that was about it. If you did generate any heat, it didn't stay inside long. The wind just sucked it out." He whistles, mimicking the icy wind he remembers.

My thoughts drift back to my spacious apartment in Vancouver: a twenty-third-floor beauty with a sweeping view of False Creek and the city beyond. I think of my floor-to-ceiling windows, storm-sealed and double-glazed. On a cold, damp night in the city I simply turn up the gas fireplace, pour a glass of wine, and watch the wind and rain lash the windows while I sit inside, warm and dry. I cringe when I think how the thin plywood walls of the granary must have rattled as the wind howled outside. And I think of those boys, tightly bundled under blankets in an attempt to stay warm.

"Father rigged up an old cookstove that allowed us to cook and gave us reasonable heat for a couple of hours," Dad told me. "After the last embers faded, we were on our own. The water in the bucket would be frozen solid by morning." Dad can sense what I'm thinking: what about those late-night trips to answer the call of nature? "Plumbing?" Dad roars. "Never heard of it. Outside, son, and you'd better move. It was bloody cold out there."

True to form, Dad always focuses on the positives: "We were young and it was somewhat of an adventure, so we really didn't think much of it. Plus, there was an outdoor skating rink just across the road from the school," he recalls. "We would hang a lantern at each end of the rink and skate long into the evenings."

Dad graduated from Northern Light High School in June of 1939. That summer, he enrolled in a year-long teacher training program at the Saskatchewan Normal School. Our young farm boy was headed for the big city: Saskatoon—the Paris of the Prairies.

When Dad puts his mind to something, he usually does well. That year, he ended up with high enough marks that he earned his teaching diploma after only a single year of study. In September of 1940, at the age of nineteen, he accepted his first placement, to teach in a one-room schoolhouse near Quill Lake, Saskatchewan, where he taught primary classes to twenty-five students of mixed grade levels.

His pay for that year was $700—a decent wage for a starting teacher in rural Saskatchewan, but still not much. It was just enough to live on, if you scrimped here and there. But there was no chance to save any money. The next year he moved to Landis, a farming settlement some 130 kilometres west of Saskatoon, to teach high school.

In the early 1940s, the cycle of a Prairie teacher's life mirrored that of the farming community they served. Today, schoolchildren attend classes that run from the beginning of September through till the start of summer in late June. But structuring the educational system like that makes no sense to a farmer, someone who plants seeds in early spring and harvests crops in late fall. Back then, it was sowing and reaping—not schooling—that dictated the ebb and flow of Prairie life.

The problem with school starting in September was that most of his class was on call, waiting for the shimmering wheat fields to signal that it was harvest time. Harvest is the highlight of a farmer's year, the time to reap a year's worth of work in a few weeks. Many of Dad's students were there for the opening of the school year, but Mother Nature dictated how long it would be until they were needed in the fields or in the family kitchen helping to bring in the sheaves—bundles of grain tied together and stacked side by side like miniature golden towers.

A multi-grade teacher in a country schoolhouse already has enough juggling to do, but factoring in harvest time presented an additional challenge. How do you create multiple-grade lesson plans for students exhausted from helping out with the family's harvest? More importantly, how do you keep them awake and alert enough to learn? The arrival of spring would set another cycle in motion when it was time to plant the seeds that would grow into fields of gold. Such was the cycle of life on the Prairies, and Dad understood that rhythm intimately.

Everything changed when the Second World War broke out. In 1939, the world watched as Hitler's army swept across the European continent. Historical allegiances with Britain drew Canada into the conflict. Many of Dad's friends had enlisted in the Armed Forces, but he was unable to enlist because he had contracted polio in his early childhood that partially impaired movement in his right arm. Wanting to contribute in some way to the war effort, he discovered that the Canadian government was heavily promoting studies in engineering and sciences, so he enrolled at the University of Saskatchewan in Saskatoon in 1941 to study math and physics.

But Dad didn't find his calling in the laboratory or see it on the blackboard. "As I got deeper into these fields," he told me, "I found that I had made a mistake. I was an average mathematician and less than average physicist. Once in the upper-level classes, the bright students destined for graduate studies really started to stand out . . . and it was obvious I wasn't part of that group."

Despite this realization, he dedicated himself to finishing the program. In 1945, Rankin Hodgins graduated with a BA in math and physics. But Dad was already looking around to see what other career choices were available. "Something less abstract than formulas and equations scrawled out on the chalkboard," he recalls.

I laugh at this suggestion. "Dad, you've become a very successful investor because you understand how to use mathematical principles to your advantage. Your investment strategy has been based on borrowing money to invest. Surely understanding how interest accumulates is important?"

Dad shrugs. "That doesn't require advanced-level university mathematics, Douglas," he says with a sheepish grin. "You of all people should know that."

"But you obviously thought it was important that your children get a post-secondary education," I respond. "You and Mom saved endlessly to ensure that all five of us had enough money..."

"So you could study business," Dad interjects. "There's a big difference."

"Okay, Dad," I concede. "I certainly appreciate the knowledge that my commerce degree gave me. It introduced me to a whole new world of ideas and concepts that have served me well in the world of personal finance."

Dad is waiting to see what I say next, because he knows I can't just leave it at that. "But it seems that you haven't done too badly for yourself, despite your lack of a finance degree," I say, gently goading him to respond.

"I think I've done alright," he replies. That brings a little smile to his face, just like I knew it would.

Chapter 5

Family & Working Life

MY DAD WAS RAISED TO VALUE EDUCATION. When you picture his father—my grandfather—hauling that granary to the lot next to the schoolhouse so the boys could stay motivated in school, the message is pretty clear. Dad's belief in the importance of education is what motivated him to enter teacher training—to pass on the joys of learning to the next generation of students.

But Dad was also a firm believer that an education should have practical value, that it should contribute in some way "to real life in the real world," as he put it. That's probably why he wasn't drawn to the abstract world of mathematical equations and the nebulous theories behind physics. He was a small-town boy who was looking for work that would allow him to contribute to his community.

He found what he was looking for at the Continental Life Insurance Company. In the summer of 1944, the branch manager of the Regina office for Continental, Bill Johnson, decided to take a chance on a young man and hired my dad as a trainee. My grandfather had been a client of Mr. Johnson, so Wilfred convinced him to hire Dad to work in the Saskatoon office. That first summer, he earned $800, which was more than he had earned for an entire year of teaching a few short years earlier.

Dad jumped at the chance to join the insurance profession. Here was a business that relied heavily on numbers, but one that used numbers to develop policies that had a real impact on the lives of people in his community. Eight months later, he reported for work at the Saskatoon office. The day after his final exams were finished, Dad wrote his first life insurance contract on April 15, 1945, one week into his new career. He stayed with the Saskatoon branch until the fall of 1948, when he was promoted to manager of the Regina office.

Soon after Dad received the transfer, his life changed again. An old teaching buddy, Jimmy Carr, was now the principal of a small school in Pelly, near the Manitoba-Saskatchewan border. Dad, who did business in small communities all over the province, met up with Jimmy one afternoon. Jimmy told Dad he had a teacher on his staff who might be of interest to him: a pretty young woman named Daphne Rosabella Louise Dundas. Initially, Dad took care of her life insurance needs. But it soon became evident he was interested in providing for her future in another way.

Once Dad decided Daphne was the right woman, he didn't waste any time. He proposed, and they were married less than a year later. They were both eager to start a family. Bill was born in 1950, Douglas in 1953 and Robert in 1954—proving again that, once Dad makes a decision, he's all in.

With three young boys and a wife to look after, Dad started to have serious doubts about the amount of travel his job demanded. On hearing that a general insurance agency was up for sale in Tisdale, 175 miles due north and 23 miles to the east of Regina, he made the trip north and quickly decided he liked what he saw. Ike Struthers owned the agency but was looking to retire. He eagerly accepted Dad's cash offer of $7,500 for the agency, so my parents immediately started planning for their future in northeastern Saskatchewan.

Tisdale was not far from where Dad had grown up. It was a small community of about 2,500 people, and my parents thought it would be a good place to raise their family. So on August 1, 1954, we began our new life in our new home, trading in the big-city lights of Regina for small-town Saskatchewan. The man who had established his career in the urban world was returning to his rural roots.

Dad remembers that the new couple and their three little boys were warmly welcomed into Tisdale. It wasn't long before Mom and Dad were active in business, church and social activities in the town. I don't remember the birth of my sister Valerie in 1959, but I definitely recall the day my father told us we had a new baby brother, John, born in 1963—their second child to have Tisdale on their birth certificate.

Life in Tisdale was good. It was a service centre for agriculture, acting as a hub for farmers up to thirty miles away. Dad's general insurance business expanded and thrived. Towns like Tisdale lived and died by the farmers. If the crop failed, the whole town suffered. And if there was a bumper crop, the town was a beehive of economic activity.

The realization of how interconnected everything is (and how interdependent everyone is) meant that everyone in small-town Saskatchewan looked out for the interests of everyone else. As a resident of Vancouver, a metropolis of more than 2 million people, I always think back about the time I spent growing up in

Tisdale. Although my parents left Tisdale for Alberta forty years ago and I don't get back there often, if anyone asks where I'm from, I never say Alberta, where my parents spent most of their lives and where my dad still lives. I'm from Tisdale, Saskatchewan, the town where I grew up and which I still proudly call my hometown.

Something about small-town life still runs in my blood. Maybe it is the feeling of mutual reciprocity a small town offers, where life can't work any other way. Everyone cares about the whole community's well-being because . . . well, they can't afford not to care. Maybe I admire the way small towns cause people to be proud of their community, fostering a level of civic engagement no urban area can match.

Town life became central to Dad's life. He met daily with business colleagues and friends at the local coffee shop on Main Street—aptly named "The Coffee Shop." You know the kind of place: one of those small-town diners with booths along a window and a long Formica countertop if you wanted to "belly up" to the lunch counter. We kids loved to spin around on those stainless steel stools with the red vinyl seats. The Coffee Shop was the place for the townsfolk to catch up. Over several cups, conversations might bounce between local, national and international news, but would always return to how this year's crop was shaping up.

Over time, Dad realized he was spending a lot of time discussing the affairs of Tisdale with his friends and business colleagues. So in 1963 he ran for town council—and was elected. In 1965, Bob Hill, the local undertaker, dropped by Dad's office to encourage him to run for mayor. Initially, he brushed it off, but Bob confided to Dad that he was the choice of "the boys on coffee row." They liked the fact that Dad knew his way around Regina, the capital of the province and place where municipal-provincial decisions were made. In the fall of 1965, Dad became mayor of Tisdale. He was re-elected in 1967.

As the '60s gave way to the '70s, my parents began to tire of the long northern-Saskatchewan winters. They decided that Dad would start looking at opportunities in Alberta and B.C. In 1973, Dad learned that a general insurance agency was for sale in southwestern Alberta. After several scouting trips and more than a few sleepless nights pondering the future of the family, Mom and Dad made the decision to move west, just like Dad's father had done in 1918. It was not the same scale of a move as Grandfather had undertaken, but a difficult move all the same. They were leaving a town that had treated them well—a town that had truly become home.

But Dad was always looking forward, and to him, the move made sense. So he sold his share of the Tisdale agency to his partner Larry Baird and bought an insurance agency in Claresholm, Alberta, where rolling pasture land gives way to the foothills of the Rockies and the snow-capped mountain peaks beyond. They built a comfortable bi-level bungalow and settled into small-town living, Alberta style.

The "three little boys of 1954" were now all enrolled in commerce at the University of Saskatchewan in Saskatoon, so didn't make the move west to Alberta with the family. My older brother Bill was nearly finished his degree, my younger brother Robert was just finishing his first year, and I had just finished my second year. Yes, you read that right. Three brothers, three commerce students. Bill graduated in 1974. I graduated two years later, in 1976, followed by Robert in 1977. Dad must have conveyed some powerful subliminal messages about business and finance as we were growing up. How else can you explain why three independent-minded young men ended up at the same university, all studying commerce?

Dad had not only worked very hard at his business in Tisdale, he had also been at the centre of civic life for nearly a decade. When he moved to Claresholm, he decided to take life a little easier by not getting so heavily involved in the community.

But taking it easier didn't mean he stopped looking for new opportunities. In 1977, Dad invited my brother Bill to join his business, and together they expanded, opening a new branch in Market Mall in northwest Calgary, which Bill ran until he switched into the investment business in the mid-'80s.

Another opportunity to expand came Dad's way: the chance to purchase an insurance agency in Cochrane, a satellite city on the Old Banff Coach Road just outside of Calgary. Dad and my sister Valerie bought the business in 1980. Valerie managed the office until 1982, when she married Mike Lowen and moved to Fort Macleod, before eventually settling in Lethbridge in 1985.

My parents retired in 1986. They stayed in Claresholm for a year, but soon realized they wanted to be closer to Valerie, Mike and their grandchildren. So in 1988, they moved to Lethbridge as well, where they enjoyed almost twenty years of retirement together until my mother passed away in 2006.

Today, at the ripe old age of ninety-one, my dad has just recently moved in with my sister Valerie. He stayed in his home as long as he could but even with a live-in caregiver, it made more sense for him to be with Valerie. When we were making that decision I asked if he would ever consider moving to a retirement or assisted living home. "I suppose," he replied, "but you'd have to drag me out of here kicking and screaming." That's Dad for you, still proud and fiercely independent after all these years.

Chapter 6

Save Your Money

I AM SITTING ON THE BACK PORCH, WAITING FOR DAD TO COME OUT. He has gone down to his office in the basement, looking for some newspaper clippings he wanted to show me. We've been talking about my book project for several hours now. I've got so many ideas bouncing around my head that I can't visualize how I can put it all together. But I sure like the direction our discussion has taken us.

Even though I've had the chance to think about book themes and lay out some structure in the two months since my last visit here in June of 2010, there's still lots of material to cover. I take a deep breath and try to stop my thoughts for a second. The dry, sweet smell of day-old cut grass hangs in the air. I hear some kids down the block squealing as they run through a sprinkler. It's a typical Alberta summer day. In Vancouver, whenever the sun shines I always try to get myself down to the ocean, or least within view of the water. I've fallen in love with the way the late-afternoon sun sparkles on the sea. But whenever I leave the coast and fly over the Rocky Mountains to visit Dad, it only takes a single sight such as a grain truck pulling into a grain elevator or the sound of crickets to remind me of my Prairie roots.

The screen door creaks open. Dad steps outside. He turns, then moves slightly to the side so he can let the door close without banging shut. He got into this habit when he and Mom moved here. She didn't like how the screen door would slam if you let it go. He always told Mom that it would be easy to fix, but I think over the years he just got used to how it closed and never did get it fixed.

I watch Dad slowly make his way over to his chair. It's more of a shuffle than anything else, a far cry from the brisk pace I remember trying to keep up to on the rare occasions he would take me to his office as a small boy. He sits down and rocks back in one slow motion. "Did you find the clipping?" I ask. "No," he replies. "But I remember what it was about."

"Douglas," he begins. "There's something I need to get off my chest." I rock back in my chair, reach up and scratch my ear. "Okay, Dad. What is it?"

He stops rocking and leans forward. "This is going to be a book about investing, right? From what you've told me, the main focus is my experiences with leveraging, what's worked and what hasn't worked, correct?"

"That's right, Dad," I reply. "We talked about how your story might be inspirational . . ." I pause momentarily. But he's not finished.

"That's just the thing, Douglas. I'm worried that with all this focus on leveraging, we might just miss—or, more accurately, you might forget to discuss—the most important point of all." He smiles as he says this, like he is foreshadowing something he's been keeping from me this whole time. "You might call it, well, the bedrock of my financial philosophy." He clasps the arms of the rocking chair with both hands and uses them to hoist himself more upright.

I take the bait, as usual. "So what are we talking about, Dad? What's the bedrock of your 'financial philosophy'?" I make quotation marks in the air with my fingers as I say this, teasing him a bit. I'm trying to anticipate what he is going to say. I'm wondering if he's trying to get in a little jab at me somehow. Then I look at him.

Dad's face has changed. He looks serious. "I'm flattered you want to share my story with whoever reads your book, but I don't want people thinking all they have to do is go out and borrow money, throw it at the stock market and presto"—he snaps his fingers—"they become instant millionaires." He wags his finger.

"Too many people are looking for an easy way to make money," he continues, "and I don't want this book to feed into that. A lot of things can go wrong with a leveraging program. You know that as well as I do." He turns his head so he can look at me straight on.

The "You know that as well as I do" is Dad's way of acknowledging the large part John and I played in rescuing his portfolio back in late 2008 and 2009. It represents the gratitude he felt when we would take his 6:00 a.m. phone calls, morning after morning—calls that we dreaded but answered anyway. "You know that as well as I do" is essentially Dad's way of thanking me. I look back at him, meet his gaze just for a second—long enough for him to convey what needs to be said.

Having received my acknowledgement, Dad drops his eyes. He scratches his chin and clears his throat. "And, from time to time, one or another of those things that can go wrong *will* go wrong, at least for a little while," he says. "This game isn't for everyone, Douglas." He squirms in his chair, his elbows straining to hold himself upright as he waits for me to respond. "So you wouldn't recommend leveraging for any and all Canadians?" I ask. I meant the question rhetorically, but he answers anyway. "No, Douglas, I certainly wouldn't," he says quietly. "In fact, I gather that many Canadians out there—especially the younger ones—won't necessarily like what I have to say about personal finance, but . . ."

"But you'll say it anyways, right?" I interject. "That's you, Dad. Never one to beat around the bush." I just let the words hang and wait for him to reply.

"Douglas," he says, "my biggest concern is that people have forgotten how to save money." He leans forward in his chair. As he does this, his glasses slip down his nose slightly, and he glares at me over the frames. I remember this look from when I was young. We probably all do, in fact: that penetrating look we got from one of our parents when we were about to be scolded or chastised for some misdeed. I always got this look from my dad. If the look was strong enough, especially in public, the message could be conveyed and fully understood without words.

"Everyone is spending beyond their means, living lives their incomes can't support. Governments are the worst offenders, spending like drunken sailors on shore leave. They aren't showing any leadership whatsoever, no responsibility to get their fiscal house in order. It's as if nobody remembers how to say no anymore. If the people want it, give it to them, whether it's fiscally prudent or not! Whatever happened to the old-fashioned principle of spending within your means?" He pauses for breath. His elderly lungs are struggling to keep up with the pace of his thoughts.

I grimace. Dad has a good point. But as I'm listening, I'm also editing. I figure I'm going to have to tone down this part.

He sounds too much like a soapbox preacher. Besides, it is pretty obvious, isn't it? Save, don't spend—pretty straightforward. But my face gives away my thoughts, and Dad jumps right in. He's not going to let anyone off the hook that easy.

"Why do these people need to have the very best of everything—and have it yesterday?" He slaps the arm of the chair, then puts his left hand on his thigh and leans forward one more time. "Remember when young couples used to save money for a few years to put a down payment on a 'starter' home? Nowadays they don't even build 'starter' homes. Now young people not only need a fancy new state-of-the-art home"—he enunciates these words slowly, the way people ask for a triple-shot skinny soy latte at their local coffee shop—"but they need expensive furnishings and the latest in stainless steel appliances." He says "stainless steel appliances" in a way that makes such modern conveniences sound like "luxuries," on par with limousines and champagne oysters on the half shell (though Mom certainly loved the stainless steel dishwasher Dad broke down and bought for her back in 2003 as a Mother's Day gift).

"Furthermore, once they get their fancy new home, they don't even stay there." Dad makes a clicking sound with his tongue, as if to chastise these big spenders. "They're not in their home more than ten minutes and they start planning for an expensive winter vacation, all the while using more credit to pay for their fancy lifestyles. In my day, if I got a trip to Regina or Saskatoon, let me tell you, that was a pretty special occasion."

As Dad says this, I think back to the recent trip I took to Brazil (to write this book, of course!). Although it wasn't cheap, I consider it a worthwhile investment in my mental health. Okay, I admit I've got the travel bug and love to explore different countries and learn about new cultures, languages and people. Besides, if we Vancouverites don't get away from the dark, dreary and rainy days of November and December, it can get to be a long, wet winter. The way I look at it, this is what life is all about: enjoying the fruits of your labour without worry or guilt. But there's no way I'm going to pipe up about it now, especially given the mood Dad's in at the moment. He has lectured me in the past on my "unnecessary" travel, lumping me in with those "big spenders" he likes to rant about and parody in equal measure.

The thing is, I totally understand what he's getting at. He's right, and I know it. In fact, we all know it. Each time we check our monthly statements and see the bills piling up, we know it. Folks like my dad—those who came of age during the Great Depression—take one look at people who max out credit cards and shake their heads. Investing in your future is one thing, Dad might say, but buying a $600 Gucci handbag or a $300 pair of sunglasses? Now that's pure indulgence.

"In my day," Dad says, "a man who spent his money like a fool was called a fool. And quite rightly so, because no one really had any money to spend on anything much more than the bare essentials. They had to think of their family, their farm, their future. But nowadays, everyone, including government, tends to spend money they don't have, and then they fall all over themselves telling anyone who will listen that it's okay." He shakes his head in disgust. "I just don't understand how some people think."

I chuckle a bit to myself. When I think about it, Dad's probably right on this one. He's still intuitively sharp and even though he doesn't always say a lot, he picks up on a lot of things. But when it comes to understanding the behavioural patterns of people he disapproves of, he rarely minces his words. I don't want to present him as being narrow-minded, because he isn't. He's open to just about anything, except irresponsibility. The way Dad sees it, people who can't manage their spending must have something "wrong" with them, as if there's some cognitive defect preventing them from managing their finances better. And that's where Dad and I differ, at least a little bit.

Now don't get me wrong. I understand precisely what Dad is saying. But I know enough about life (and enough about people) to know that some people don't always spend as wisely as they should. Human beings are governed by many emotions other than what looks good on paper or is rational. Sure, the "I've got to have it now" mentality has been heavily promoted and perpetuated by marketing firms and slick advertising campaigns. Clearly they don't have to twist our collective arms too hard in order to separate us from the dollars we work so hard to earn.

Fast-food restaurants have made millions—billions, in fact—by upselling customers, suggesting French fries to those customers who hadn't even considered ordering them a minute earlier. Cold beer and wine stores charge higher prices because they know there are people who can't plan far enough ahead to buy and chill the beer the day before the backyard barbecue. Credit card companies are more than happy to continue loaning millions of dollars at exorbitant interest rates to people who really ought to quit spending cold turkey. The underlying premise of today's consumer-debt economy—that "you can wait and save . . . or you can pay more and get it right now"—wouldn't gain traction if there weren't millions of people who can't seem to say no to easy and, may I say, very expensive credit.

I want to say all this to Dad, but I don't. Because ultimately, he's right. People are spending beyond their means, living lives they can't afford. But they aren't being tricked into spending money. No one honestly believes they can somehow afford those nice leather sofas on an "easy layaway plan" when they're already behind on their hydro bill. There's no question we're all tempted by easy credit but the people who dive in and overspend are really only fooling themselves.

Dad clears his throat again. "There's no point me promoting more aggressive investment and tax planning strategies if people haven't mastered the basic art of saving their money, living within their means, and having a few dollars left over to invest in their future. Although we can't take it with us, I can't think of anyone who doesn't want to retire with at least some level of comfort and dignity—we don't stay young forever, you know."

A few years ago, Dad gave a very similar speech to Ken Corba, my Wall Street money manager friend. Over the years, Ken has taken a keen interest in my dad's financial affairs. Whenever we chat on the phone, Ken always wants to know how his portfolio is doing. By 2005 he was so intrigued by Dad's strategy that he requested a copy of the spreadsheet so he could independently track Dad's finances. Dad proudly sent it off and they've been comparing notes ever since.

Anyway, Ken eventually decided that he had to meet my dad, face to face. Dad was a little intimidated to hit the bright lights of New York City, so they agreed to meet in LA—Lethbridge, Alberta. Ken walked through the front door, met both my parents, and then told Dad he wanted to see this "nerve centre" in the basement that he'd been hearing so much about. As they descended the stairs, Ken teased Dad, telling him that he was planning on building a home office himself and needed some tips on how to keep the costs down. When they got to the bottom of the stairs, Dad slapped Ken on the back and said he already liked how he thought. "Mr. Corba, I can see right now that you and I are going to get along just fine."

I should mention that one of Ken's greatest attributes is that he seems like a serious guy—until he opens his mouth. He loves to get a dig into everyone he meets, so over dinner he was needling Dad about how well he must be treating my mother, given his investment success. "I would imagine that you've been treating Daphne to all the finest in diamonds, jewels and furs, now that you're making all this money, Rankin," Ken said slyly, glancing over at my mother. The look on my mother's face was priceless. Even though the question had been directed at my father, it was too much for my otherwise tactful mother to resist. She interrupted, extending her left hand with bare fingers across the table, and said: "You see these fancy rings? Rankin says nothing is too good for me . . . and that's exactly what I've got!"

Later that evening, Ken goaded Dad even further. "Rankin," he said, "let me tell you something about us New York City finance guys. When we make money, we make big money. But when we spend money, we spend big money. You know," Ken leaned in, as if he was letting Dad in on a secret, "the last time I entertained your sons at my favourite lunch spot in New York, I paid $12 for a bottle of water. What do you think of that?"

Dad didn't miss a beat. "Mr. Corba," he said, "did I just hear you say *$12 for a bottle of water?*" Ken nodded. "That's right, Rankin, $12." Dad was incredulous. He cleared his throat, looked Ken directly in the eye—and said very dryly, "Well, I think someone should introduce you to a tap." Ken smiled mischievously, which sent Dad the signal he wanted. "Mr. Corba?" Dad responded, extending his hand. "My name is Faucet, Mr. Faucet to you. I think we need to get a little better acquainted." We all had a big laugh over that one.

If there is one thing you can say about Dad, he sure has guts. I mean, here's one of the "big boys" of the New York financial world—someone Dad has looked up to for years—sitting at his dinner table, and what does he do? No hero worship. Dad gives Ken the "big spender" treatment, right to his face. I don't think I'll ever forget that moment. But if I ever do, I suspect I can always count on Ken to remind me of it.

Chapter 7

The Magic of
Compound Interest

THE SUN IS SINKING LOWER NOW, SETTING THE ALBERTA SKY ABLAZE WITH COLOUR. The wind rustles the branches of the trees that shade Dad's back porch. We've been throwing ideas around for most of the afternoon, but I sense that Dad is wearing out as he's not used to this much stimulation all at once. And to be honest, I'm also getting tired. I'm the guy, after all, who has to sit down later on and put all our ideas into some semblance of order. Dad just gets to sit back and let the words tumble out, pontificating about something that he's truly passionate about.

"There are only two things people need to know before they start investing," Dad says. He likes to phrase things in little lists sometimes, talking about the "three basic principles" or the "two most important rules." Some people think he does this because he's full of himself or thinks he's pretty smart. But this is just how his mind works. He is most comfortable laying things out in a logical manner. This way, there's not much chance of him being misunderstood.

"First, they need to understand how compound interest works," he says. "And that will make the second thing really obvious." I nod. "Okay," I say slowly, helping him set up for his next line. "What's the second thing?"

"Second," he adds, "they will realize they should have started investing a decade ago." He looks over, waiting for my reaction. I can tell he's been thinking about that one for a while now.

"That's going in the book," I say, offhandedly. He smiles. "Good idea, Douglas, but I'm going to have to call it a night," he says, rising from his rocking chair. "I'll be a lot better in the morning after a decent night's sleep."

~

Understand compound interest and you understand what drives wealth creation. Everything Dad has accomplished over the years stems from the fact that he understands the power of compounding. Einstein famously called compound interest the "eighth wonder of the world," saying simply: "He who understands it, earns it . . . and he who doesn't, pays it." Dad has always insisted that he wasn't much of a math student at university, but he obviously managed to pick up a reasonable understanding of this basic concept. It's one of his favourite subjects. Over the years he's talked about it with anyone who would listen and probably plenty of others who didn't want to listen.

I made a point to get up early today but can't match Dad's enthusiasm to get going again. I manage to hold him off while I have my breakfast but realize there's no point in even considering reading the paper. He joins me at the table and starts right in. "Douglas, this little gem is the first thing that you need to understand before starting any kind of a savings or investment program. Compounding occurs when interest, dividends or capital gains are added to your original sum invested. This creates a larger capital base for all future growth to occur on. Everything we do in the investment world should be organized to take advantage of this single principle. Every investor's goal should be to reinvest all earnings along with any income taxes saved or deferred to maximize their capital base, which, of course, maximizes the future growth of their portfolio. The power of this simple concept is staggering."

Dad stops for a moment. "Have you seen the compound interest chart I keep down in my office?" He looks up at me but doesn't give me a chance to answer. "Come on," he says as he motions for me to follow him. "It's time for my compound interest pitch."

"Give me a minute to finish my tea, Dad," I plead. He grunts. "Well, hurry up, this is important stuff. If you don't understand this, then you won't understand anything else I tell you later on." I roll my eyes. I think Dad sometimes forgets that he's shown me this chart dozens of times over the years or that I have a commerce degree and more than thirty years of experience in the financial planning world. But I always enjoy how animated he gets giving me the "compound interest pitch," so I go along with it one more time.

One thing you have to know about my dad is that he loves charts and numbers. The other thing you have to know about him is that he loves to keep ahead of the curve, trying to get an "edge on everybody else," as he likes to say. Did I mention that he also likes to be in charge? Big surprise, right? Even at his age, he still enjoys "holding court" in his basement office. Anyway,

Dad pulls out his compound interest chart that he still keeps in the top left-hand drawer of his desk. It's tattered and torn, having been through countless presentations to family members over the years.

"Okay, let me give you a few of the basics here, Douglas," he says as he starts his presentation. "Let's assume that you invest $1,000 in a GIC and earn a 2% annual return that you reinvest back into your GIC every year." He slowly but adeptly runs his finger down ten years on the 2% column and says: "There it is, your $1,000 has grown to $1,220. Not bad, but it's pretty tough to build a decent retirement income on a 2% return. Now let's increase your compound return to 6%." His finger slides along, stopping at $1,790. "A little better," he continues, "but personally I like to earn at least 10%. If I can get that, I increase my ten-year compound return to $2,590. Now we're talking my kind of language."

I've heard this presentation before. In fact, I pretty much have it memorized. So as Dad launches into his twenty-year returns, my mind starts to wander, taking me back to previous visits.

November 22, 2004. The day dawned crisp and abnormally cold, considering it was only late November. I was visiting my parents in Lethbridge to celebrate Dad's eighty-third birthday. The temperature was up from its nighttime low but still well below zero. As I made my way to the breakfast table, I noted that the kitchen window was fogged up.

That morning, Dad wasn't thinking much about his birthday, the temperature outside or foggy windows. He was deeply engrossed in something he'd read the evening before. He reached across the breakfast table and thrust a copy of the TD Bank's annual report under my nose. "You see?" he said. I stopped chewing. My mouth was still half-full of Mom's fluffy scrambled eggs, but I have learned over the years that when Dad is trying to tell me something, there's no point ignoring him or trying to do something else.

I remember scanning the columns, feeling a bit like this was a pop quiz to evaluate my financial abilities. "If I had invested $10,000 with TD Bank in 1960," Dad said, "do you know how much it would be worth today?" Sensing he had more to say, I sat quietly, watching the steam rise from his coffee mug as I awaited his response to what appeared to be a rhetorical question.

"Four million three hundred thousand dollars," Dad replied, "give or take." He probably would have slammed his fist down on the breakfast table if Mom hadn't been standing by the sink. "That's a compound annual return of about 16%," he roared. "A bit of leveraging would have added another 5 or 6%. Can you imagine if I had done nothing else but put every available dollar I had into TD Bank?"

I could tell that the thought of someone else making all that money—someone other than him, someone who had the foresight to get in early—was getting under his skin. And I could tell he wanted me to say something. I tried to do the calculations in my head, looking for an answer that might placate him. "Okay, Dad," I offered, "that's assuming you left the investment untouched and reinvested all the dividends . . ."

"As I always do!" he retorted. Hmm, I thought to myself, clearly this wasn't the response he was looking for. So I tried another angle. "Not many people have your discipline or persistence when it comes to thinking long term," I answered, confident that I would prove my understanding of what he had just said while at the same time stroking his ego a little bit. Besides, my eggs were getting cold. "And do you really think other investors would have been reinvesting all the dividends, every year," I went on, "without spending a cent on themselves or their family?" As I said this,

I saw Mom crack a slight smile. "You know, dear," she said over his shoulder, tenderly as always, "some people do like a holiday every now and then . . ."

It was clear she was just trying to get her "two cents" in on the matter. Dad picked up his coffee mug, raised it to his lips and, after taking a sip, slowly shook his head. "If I could give any advice," he began, which of course elicited an even bigger smile from Mom—since Dad doesn't let an opportunity slip by to give anyone within earshot a little free advice—"I would tell them to just do it," he said, slapping his hand down on the table. "Invest now. Yesterday would have been better, of course," he added, "but today will also work. Just get started as soon as you can." I looked over at Mom. She rolled her eyes, but deep down she knew he was right.

~

"So?" Dad's words snap me back into the present. I glance over and see his finger hovering over a set of figures. "Am I right?" he asks. His eyes meet mine.

I smile sheepishly and turn away. I've been caught not paying attention. Here Dad was busy talking about the benefits of compound interest, and meanwhile I've been replaying this scene from 2004 that really got me excited about examining the inter-relationships between compound interest, taxation and leverage in the creation of long-term wealth. He's holding tight to the theory behind it, while I'm already thinking about how I'm going to combine the theory of leveraging with his personal investment story to create something that readers can actually learn from while enjoying a good read.

Dad dislikes it when people don't give him their undivided attention. But there's a part of him that probably realizes his memory is not what it once was, so there's a chance, albeit a small one, that he might have already been through this with me once or twice before. That seems to temper his annoyance somewhat. Dad looks over. Seeing that he has regained my attention, he starts again.

"Okay, in case you missed it, here are the twenty-year numbers. The 2% compounded GIC grows to $1,488 but my 10% stock portfolio grows to $6,708. At thirty years the difference is even greater. But what really grabs my attention is compound interest over forty years."

"That's a long time, Dad," I respond.

"Yes, it is, but you'll see that something magical happens over this time horizon. Look at 2% money," he says. "It's grown to $2,214. Four percent money grows to $4,796 over the same time period. Six percent money grows to $10,265, and 8% money grows to $21,365. Let's take a look at 10% money. That's right, it grows to $44,998. Do you see what's happening here, Douglas?"

"Yes, as a matter of fact, I do, Dad," I answer somewhat mechanically. "The real power of compounding is best shown over a forty-year time period, where it literally 'jumps' off the chart so that every 2% increase in return doubles your money. The opposite also occurs, so that a 2% reduction in return reduces your money by half. Hmm, looks like investment return over the long term really does matter." From his face, I can tell I've passed Dad's little quiz—but my distinct lack of enthusiasm in his favourite subject fails to impress him.

"Always has, always will," Dad curtly responds. "I've been trying to tell you this for a long time, Douglas, but I'm not sure how well you've been listening."

Chapter 8

Leveraged Investing: Know All the Facts

DAD MADE ME PROMISE THIS BOOK WOULDN'T BE LIKE THE "OTHER BOOKS" ON FINANCE OUT THERE. He said he didn't want me to overwhelm people with charts and calculations. Just offer the reader simple explanations, he kept saying, and you'll have a book anyone can read.

"Do you have any idea know how many books on 'investing tips' or 'investor secrets' I've started to read but never finished, Douglas?" he asks me over breakfast the next morning. He doesn't bother to stop chewing his toast, which means he expects me to do the same. But I've just popped a forkful of eggs into my mouth, so I signal with my hand to give me a minute. He waits, but looks exasperated at how long it takes me to swallow.

"How many, Dad?" I reply. "I don't know for sure, but let's just say too many," he snaps back. "That's not the point. The point is that I never bothered to finish any of them, because they didn't tell me anything useful. Sure, they had fancy charts and graphs about some complicated financial concept that was sure to make you wealthy over a twenty-year period . . ."

"You mean," I interrupt, "like the charts you're always poring over downstairs?" Dad raises his eyebrows. "Yes, Douglas, a lot like those," he answers. "But that's not the point either. The point is"—Dad's trying to keep a straight face as he switches back to "lecture" mode—"that no one who picks up a book on investing in general—or on leveraged investing in particular—is going to care one iota about what some chart says or what some graph supposedly demonstrates. They aren't going to plunk down a twenty-dollar bill just because some mathematical calculation says it makes sense." I nod.

"People aren't stupid," he says. "Just because you caught three fish in an hour at the lake last summer doesn't mean you'll reel in six this summer if you just sit in the boat for two hours." He laughs at this. "They know the real world is a little more complicated than this."

"So how do you suggest we proceed?" I ask. Dad is quick with an answer. "Well, sooner or later somebody," he pauses, "is going to have to explain what leveraging is." He leans on his left elbow and rubs his chin. "So you'd better get to work on that, Douglas," he says, "and while you're doing that, I'll get myself another cup of coffee." He groans as he slowly raises himself up.

"Actually, I thought we could work on it together, Dad," I reply. But he's already shuffling over to the counter. I hear the spoon clink in his mug as he stirs in the sugar. Then he replies: "I just figure that's a job for the man whose name is going on the cover of the book." I start to say something, but he waves me off as he heads for the basement, off to check how the European markets are doing. So I reach across the table and grab the pad of lined paper I've been working on for the past few days. I fold over the top page, filled with sideways calculations and over-enthusiastic asterisks. Then I crease the top of the pad so I'm staring at a fresh sheet. I lean back in my chair, exhale deeply and try to focus my thoughts. Eventually I write WHAT IS LEVERAGING? in big letters across the top of the page.

What is leveraging?

In finance, the term *leveraging* describes the process of adding borrowed capital to an investor's capital to amplify the investor's gains and losses. The amount of amplification is dictated by the ratio of borrowed capital to investor capital. For example, a 40/60 ratio of borrowed capital to investor capital will yield greater amplification than a 25/75 ratio. Therefore, the key to leveraging success is to find the "sweet spot"—the ideal ratio of borrowed capital to investor capital—that produces the returns you are seeking at a level of risk you're comfortable with.

After I've been writing for about ten minutes. I stop, pen poised, waiting for the next word, but nothing seems to come. I look up and notice that Dad has returned to the kitchen. Can't be much happening with the European markets, I think to myself, otherwise Dad would have said something to me. He's over at the counter, but I'm not sure what he's doing. There's no food in front of him, the kettle is off, and there's no mug out. Maybe Dad went over there for something and then forgot what he started out to do. It's happening more these days, this forgetting where he's going or what he's doing. It forces me to acknowledge that he's getting older. He's been around for more than nine decades, so I can't help but think that now is a great time to be working on this story . . . because I can foresee a time when he won't be here and it will be just me, writing a story about him—using the past tense. That's what's great about today. We're in the present tense.

"Hey, Dad," I call out. "Let me read this back to you. I just wrote it now, kind of rough, but at least it's a working definition." His head turns slightly towards me but he has a puzzled look on his face—which means he didn't really hear me. I get up from the table and walk over. I put my hand on his shoulder and lean in. "Come over here for a minute, Dad, I've got something to show you," I say to him. "I'd like to read you the bit I wrote on leveraging to see what you think." He nods, and I help him get seated at the kitchen table.

Using "other people's money" to make you money

Now Dad's sitting across from me. I read him my leveraging definition. When I'm done, he frowns and gets a look on his face like he's really mulling it over. I put the notepad down. "So," I inquire, "what do you think? Do you like it? Is it concise enough for you?" Dad doesn't give compliments readily, so I'm hamming it up a bit to convince him that my definition can work.

He scratches his chin. "You know, I figure it's just too darn complicated, Douglas," he answers. "Going to go over lots of people's heads, for sure." He nods as he says this. "What was that bit about 'the amplification is dictated by the ratio' or something like that? Do you expect people to pay you good money just so you can confuse them?"

I go quiet for a moment. I reread my definition, and I like it. But maybe he's right. It might be too complicated. "Okay, Dad, why don't you take a run at it? But keep it simple."

"Alright, Douglas, I will." He draws in a deep breath. "I think of leveraging as the process of using 'other people's money' to help me make money." He slaps his hand on the placemat. "And that's the simplest damned version you'll ever get."

I think it over, then shrug. "You're right, Dad," I say. "That is the simplest damned version," I concede, "except who are these 'other people' you are talking about? I mean, I know what you're getting at—you mean the bank, and maybe the taxman, if you play your cards right—but really, who else thinks about leveraged investing like this? You're going to scare off readers if they think you're advocating borrowing from the Mob or something like that." I say this just to be a little controversial. It works.

"Okay, Douglas," he says, more sternly. "How about this? You write that I said the first thing people need to do is to find a good solid investment they can trust," he says. "Then, if they think it's a safe enough investment for their own money, tell them that the second thing they should do is to add in some borrowed capital as well." He chuckles. "No sense letting all that potential compound return go to waste, after all. And the third thing to do," he lets this one hang a bit longer, pausing as he often does for effect, "is to sit back and enjoy the feeling you get, rerouting tax dollars destined for Ottawa back into your own pocket." The look on his face as he says this reflects the obvious contentment he gets from this part of the process.

How it works

In reality, Dad's definition is correct: leveraging essentially is using "other people's money" to make more money for yourself. Dad has used a small amount of his money ($200,000), along with the bank's money and the government's money in the form of actual taxes saved and unrealized capital gains taxes deferred to the future, to create a $7-million nest egg over the past thirty-five years. In addition, he's been able to gift $2 million to his family as part of a pre-estate distribution plan. Want to know the best thing about all this? He's done all this essentially using "other people's money."

"Okay, Dad," I announce. "It's decided. Your definition is going to be the one we use for the book." He grins. "I knew you'd like it," he says. "But," I add, "we have to clarify a few things. You know, help people really understand the concept. Some actual numbers, percentages, tax savings—you know what I mean." He shrugs and says, "I think the best way to approach this is to give them a simple example of how it works. Do you have your pad of paper handy?

"Okay, let's assume someone—Investor One, let's just call him Bert—invests $1,000 and earns a 10% return. That's $100 from their investment. Got it?" I nod. "Now, let's further assume that Bert is in a 40% marginal tax bracket [Note: marginal tax bracket is the percentage paid on an investor's last dollar of income] so the tax bill is $40 on his $100 of earnings. That leaves $60 in after-tax cash flow, or a 6% net return. Are you with me, Douglas?" My forehead furrows as I concentrate on getting this down. Dad will insist that I read this all back to him, and if it isn't precisely the way he worded it, he gets slightly perturbed, thinking I may be editing his words on the fly or trying to "improve" his presentation.

"Okay, now let's look at Investor Two, who I'll call Gladys. She decides to invest the same $1,000 and is in the same 40% marginal tax bracket. But Gladys decides to also borrow $1,000 to create $2,000 of invested capital. Okay, now let's assume the annual borrowing cost—the interest expense—is 6%, or $60 for the year.

"Gladys is receiving $200 of earnings, based on a 10% return on the $2,000 investment.

"But Gladys needs to pay for the cost of borrowing the $1,000, right?" I interject. I know the answer already, but I just say this to move the conversation along. Dad's eyes light up. Now he's getting to his favourite part. "Well, not exactly. Yes, Gladys has to pay the $60 interest cost up front, but remember that the interest cost is tax deductible against all other sources of income, so the government will give her back a $24 [$60 × 40%] tax refund when she files her income tax return, so her real interest cost is only $36."

Dad carries on, "For the purposes of calculating Gladys's taxable income and tax payable, here's how I see it. Gladys has $200 of income and $60 of tax-deductible interest, leaving taxable income of $140. She pays tax on 40% of this income. How much is that, Douglas?" Before I can answer Dad says, "It's $56, so by my count that means that she has net after-tax income of ... let's see ... that must make it $84, or an 8.4% return on her $1,000 investment.

"How much did we say Bert's after-tax return was, Douglas?" Dad asks. I shake my writing hand, pen in hand, and respond. "Sixty dollars, Dad," I answer, pretending to read it back to him, even though I'm reciting it from memory.

"Okay, I make that a difference of $24. Have I lost you, son?" he says with a grin. "Not yet, Dad," I reply, as I reach for my calculator. I peck a few numbers in, just for show. "Looks like Gladys got an additional 2.4% after-tax return on her money over Bert's 6%," Dad says, "and we haven't taken into account the additional tax savings associated with dividends and capital gains over interest income. However, that will have to wait for another discussion, as I want to keep this example simple and straightforward."

Dad continues, "Now, if Gladys stays patient, doesn't get greedy, and is willing to talk in terms of decades rather than years, then she's got a nice little program going. Add two or three zeros, and now we're really talking. Remember my compound interest chart that shows how you double your money over forty years for every 2% increase in after-tax return? Well, Gladys may not have forty years, but she's clearly light-years ahead of Bert," he adds with a crafty smile.

I ponder Dad's comments for a few moments and then put pen to paper. Obviously every investor prefers to earn a higher rate of return, but the real world doesn't always work this way. And that's the part most people struggle with: trying to justify the possibility that their hard-earned investment dollars may go down in the short term before they go up. Over the long term, wise investors will only accept greater risk if they have an expectation of greater return. The opposite also holds true. Investors who are risk averse should expect lower long-term returns than their more aggressive cousins. Every investor should also know and understand that all bets are off for short-term stock market performance, where the best predictor may be the toss of a coin.

For this reason, I always tell my clients that investing and wealth accumulation involve more than just the desire to make money. It's crucial to know yourself: your goals, your time horizon and the amount of risk you're comfortable with. Once you determine this, the next step is to develop a strategy to allocate that risk to the most tax-efficient capital pools, reducing risk in less tax-efficient capital pools and increasing it in more tax-efficient pools.

This process of mapping out an investment strategy is where people like me—financial planners and advisors—can add real value for clients. We need to help them really understand all of the risks and rewards of investing and in addition, the critical role that tax minimization plays in wealth accumulation. Once clients understand these key concepts, we need to guide them in developing risk-appropriate and tax-efficient long-term investment strategies.

For instance, the low-risk, income-oriented part of an investor's portfolio should be concentrated in RRSPs and defined contribution pension plans, while higher-risk, growth-oriented investments should be concentrated in open accounts, Tax-Free Savings Accounts and leveraged accounts.

These concepts really aren't that complicated, but their impact on long-term wealth creation should never be underestimated. The key is to know how much risk you want to take in your overall portfolio and then allocate that risk to individual parts of your portfolio as efficiently as you possibly can. It sounds easy, but it's always more complicated in real life than in theory.

Why leveraging works: One simple fact

No matter what type of investments we make, whether in GICs, bonds, stocks or real estate, we always have a partner who shares in our income and gains or losses. This partner becomes more visible every April when we file our annual tax return, wanting their share of our interest, dividend income, and realized capital gains along with their normal share of our employment or self-employed income earned in the previous year. Yes, you guessed it: our partner is the Canada Revenue Agency. Bet you never thought of them as a partner before, did you?

In addition to collecting taxes on any annual taxable earnings, our tax partner is also waiting patiently for us to generate capital gains and RRIF and pension income at some point in the years ahead. How we organize our financial affairs can have a dramatic impact on how much income tax we pay, both today and in the future. The first step in learning how to play any game is to know and understand the rules. Once we know the rules inside out, we can start to develop strategies to actually win the game.

The goal of the tax game is to minimize our income taxes,

both today and in the future. Minimizing current taxes is an obvious goal, but we shouldn't underestimate the importance of deferring taxes to the future and reducing taxes in retirement. Reducing future taxes requires long-term tax planning, so the sooner we get started, the more flexibility we'll have in reducing those future tax bills.

Our partner, the CRA, asks for its share of our income in varying amounts. For example, in British Columbia, the CRA receives up to 43.7% of all employment, interest, RRIF and pension income; 25.8% of dividend income; and 21.85% of all realized capital gains generated in each tax year. As you can see, the type of income we earn makes a significant difference in determining how much tax we will actually pay, both now and in the years ahead. For example, since only 50% of capital gains are taxable, they attract only 50% the tax that is paid on employment income, pension and RRIF income, and interest earned. Tax on dividends is slightly higher, but still only about 60% of the rates charged on the aforementioned income.

So if I can show you how to decrease taxes paid on both your income today and in retirement by as much as 40 to 50%, my guess is that you'll probably want to know more. Better yet, you may even want to incorporate some of these ideas into your own planning regime.

Let's first look at the tax treatment of capital gains. The prospect of reducing your tax bill by 50% by earning capital gains rather than other income should at least have your attention. But perhaps just as important is the fact that your partner, the CRA, generously allows you to decide *when* to pay this tax. For example, my dad has racked up a future tax bill of more than a million dollars by not selling his beloved bank stocks.

The big message in retirement tax planning is that you need to start planning now. The sooner you start, the greater your planning options are to minimize taxes in retirement. You should also consider diversifying your retirement saving options as much as you can. This allows you to diversify your sources of retirement income and gain the tax flexibility associated with each option. So start early and diversify: good advice, simple but highly effective.

Don't like paying taxes? I have more good news. Do you remember that the CRA allows you to write off interest expense incurred for the purposes of generating investment income? Eligible investments for this deduction include stocks, ETFs and mutual funds that generate investment income and, of course, real estate. Interest is deductible at whatever your marginal tax rate is, so in the case of B.C. taxpayers, up to 43.7% of interest expense can be deducted against all other sources of income. What does this mean for leveraged taxpayers? It's quite simple— the more you currently pay in taxes, the greater your potential tax savings from deductible interest expenses and the greater the benefit associated with the use of this strategy.

So let's take a moment and review your relationship with the tax department. I may be repeating myself somewhat here, but this stuff can never be emphasized enough. In B.C., the CRA will share both interest income and deductible interest expenses up to a 56.3% investor / 43.7% taxman basis. Dividend income is shared on a 74.2% investor / 25.8% CRA basis. Better yet, capital gains share on a 78.15% investor / 21.85% CRA basis.

~

"Douglas," Dad interrupts me. I'm reading this section back to him at the kitchen table. "You need to red-flag this section. Make damn sure your readers understand the deal they're getting." I stop. "How do you suggest I do that, Dad?" I reply. "Oh, I don't know," he mutters. "Put it in all capital letters, maybe. That's what I used to do, back in my day." I chuckle. Dad's not really up on the Internet and the "etiquette" surrounding the use of capital letters. I gently try to fill him in. "Dad, most people avoid using all capital letters when they're online. It makes it sound like they're yelling, and that can turn some people off."

Dad snorts. "I don't have a clue what you're talking about with this 'online' business," he bellows, shaking his finger. "Furthermore, if you are telling me that this bit of tax advice isn't something worth yelling about, I don't know what the hell else is!" He slams his fist down on the table, which causes his toast crumbs to spill off his plate. I try my best but can't suppress a big smile. Dad sees this, and the tension evaporates. "Douglas, I don't care what you have to do to get the point across," he continues. "But you tell your readers that this is the best damn advice they are ever going to get . . . and for free, at that."

I raise my eyebrows. "Dad, are you planning to fund this book as a vanity project?" I ask. "If you are, that's great. I won't have to worry about recouping the costs of production, and that's one less thing for me to worry about."

Dad laughs again. "Okay, I take that back. Let's say, for the bargain price of $25. But you better make sure that this tax advice stands out. I want it in letters so big it will be visible from outer space, like that Chinese wall they always talk about." I laugh out loud. "Dad, maybe with all the profits, we could take a trip to China, to see that wall." He shakes his head. "No chance of that. But there's an excellent Chinese restaurant right here in Lethbridge, and that's as close to China as I'm going to get!"

I shrug. "Okay, Dad. I'll make sure it's clear how important that tax information is." I flip over my pad of paper and, with Dad watching, write in big letters:

STOP! GO BACK AND REREAD THE LAST FEW PARAGRAPHS. DO NOT PASS 'GO' UNTIL YOU COMPLETELY UNDERSTAND WHAT YOU'VE JUST READ. UNDERSTAND THIS CONCEPT AND YOU'LL PASS

'GO' COLLECTING $200 FOREVER. WHAT COULD BE BETTER THAN CONTROLLING THE MONOPOLY GAME IN PERPETUITY?

Dad has always loved the game *Monopoly*. Fits his character. I figure putting that reference in there will help clear this section with him. I recite back to him what I've written. Dad grunts and motions for me to continue.

ANYTIME YOU HAVE AN INVESTMENT PARTNER— IN THIS CASE, THE TAXMAN—WHO WILL SHARE THE EXPENSES AT TWICE THE RATE THEY RECEIVE ON PROFITS, YOU SHOULD JUMP ALL OVER IT! THIS SIMPLE RELATIONSHIP IS THE REASON LEVERAGED INVESTING WORKS AND SHOULD BE CONSIDERED AS AN INTEGRAL PART OF A LONG-TERM WEALTH CREATION PROGRAM.

I look over at Dad. He sticks out his chin, then scratches it carefully. "That bit's okay," he says. "But there's more, something else that's missing." I tilt my head slightly, as if to beg the question. He holds up his finger, like he's lecturing. "I'm not suggesting people should increase their overall amount of portfolio risk. And I sure as hell don't think they should be leveraging if they don't have their personal finances in good shape . . ." I see where this is headed, so I cut him off fast. "Dad," I butt in, "I think what we should say is . . ." I take the pen and start writing, with bravado:

DO WHATEVER YOU HAVE TO DO TO REDUCE RISK IN OTHER PARTS OF YOUR PORTOLIO SO YOU CAN INCLUDE AT LEAST SOME LEVERAGE IN YOUR RETIREMENT SAVINGS STRATEGY.

Then I add: DON'T INCREASE YOUR OVERALL PORTFOLIO RISK. I underline this sentence. Then I write: KEY CONCEPT— REALLOCATE RISK TO THE MOST TAX-EFFICIENT CAPITAL POOLS. I look over at Dad. He's grinning, which means he likes at least some of it. I draw in a breath. "What do you think, Dad?" I raise my eyebrows.

He nods. "I couldn't have written it better myself, Douglas. It's precisely what I was thinking." Then he drops his shoulders and snorts a breath out. "Well, son, I think we're done here." Suddenly his eyes light up. "What time is it now, Douglas?" I glance at the clock. "It's just coming up to 3:15, Dad," I reply. "Well, I'd better get moving downstairs," he says. "Howard Green has Mark Carney coming on his program at 3:30. In case you've forgotten, Douglas, he's the top dog over at the Bank of Canada, so when he speaks, guys like us should listen. Mind you, he keeps things pretty close to his chest, but you never know, he might let something slip out that really shouldn't come out. "Regardless," he says, "I like to get the news on what he's thinking on a first-hand basis." With that, Dad shuffles off towards the stairs.

I sit back and marvel at Dad's energy. It's amazing that he still wants to keep up-to-date with what's going on in the world—especially at the ripe old age of ninety-one. I sometimes wonder whether this "book thing" is too much for him, but then when I stop to think about it, this is what really keeps him going. Besides, I say to myself, he's an old farm boy, so he's used to working from dawn till dusk.

Chapter 9

Understanding
Investment Risk

"**D**AD?" I CALL OUT FROM THE TOP OF THE STAIRS. He's down in his office. "Ready to get back at it? It's time to talk risk."

I hear a grunting sound as he rises from his chair. "I'm coming, Douglas. Just hold your horses." I open the screen door and carry two glasses of lemonade out to the porch. I set Dad's glass down, slipping a paper coaster underneath it. That's Mom's influence. It used to get Dad riled up, but eventually he got used to it, and now he does it religiously, even though it's been more than six years since her passing.

A few minutes later, he appears at the door. "Okay, son, let's get started. Risks and rewards, right?" He eases into his chair.

"On the surface," Dad begins, "the list of leveraging risks is long compared to the list of benefits. When you stop to think about it, there are only two real benefits to leveraging. First, your rate of return is amplified and, given sufficient time, leveraged returns should outperform unleveraged returns. This isn't guaranteed, but given that stock markets must eventually reflect economic growth, and assuming that economic growth does occur, individual companies will eventually participate in that growth."

"Sure, Dad, but some companies will obviously do better than others in participating in that growth. So how's a novice investor supposed to choose the right companies? Think of the people who are going to be reading this book," I say. "What advice would you give to them?"

"Well," he replies, "the art of portfolio management is to pick the companies that are consistently profitable and going to grow over time. I happen to like companies that pay out a reasonable amount of their profit in the form of dividends. Something in my pocket every quarter helps me pay the banker and keeps me happy at the same time." He clears his throat.

"And the second benefit of leveraging involves reduced taxation. This is a biggie. In fact, for people in higher tax brackets, it's one of the best reasons to start leveraging," Dad says, with a flourish in his voice. "Tax-deductible interest reduces your taxable income—and, in turn, your annual tax bill. I've worked this angle pretty well over the years, sometimes paying almost nothing in taxes."

"There's one more thing folks should remember," he says, adding to his second point. "As long as you adopt a buy-and-hold strategy, taxes on your unrealized capital gains are deferred to the future. This allows compound interest to work on a larger capital base, meaning you benefit from the money staying in your pocket, earning extra return on your behalf, rather than being spent on who knows what by the government."

I look at Dad, then down at the notes in my lap. I swirl the ice cubes in my glass. Nearly empty. Got to get a refill soon. Living out on Canada's west coast, I'm no longer used to this dry Alberta heat. "Now, let's get started on that list of risks . . ." Dad hesitates for a second and changes tack. "Douglas, the one thing I would say before any of this, however, is that your readers need to do all they can to reduce the risk in other areas of their portfolio. This allows them to take on leverage risk without increasing their overall portfolio risk, which I happen to think is pretty damned important.

"You know, it's kind of funny," he says. "This morning I woke up thinking about all the risks that a leveraged investor faces. Funny, because until today I hadn't really tried to identify each and every risk. Who knows, I might never have started leveraging had I thought too much about it," he adds with a chuckle. "Luckily, I just went ahead because I believed in the numbers and figured it would work out in the end. But now that you're writing a book on the subject, I think we need to discuss all of the risks associated with the strategy. Otherwise we're not giving readers the whole story."

I reach to scratch my neck where a mosquito just landed, then reply: "Okay, Dad, I'm ready when you are." He launches into a discussion of risks, and I can quickly see that he has given the subject some serious thought. "I think you need to break risk down into two categories. The first category is normal stock market risk. And the second is the additional risks associated with leveraged investing. Since leveraging amplifies stock market gains and losses, it also amplifies normal stock market risks, especially normal investor emotional risk. I think you need to talk about these additional risks separately."

"Okay, then let's start with normal stock market risk," I say. Dad puts his hand to his chin and glances down, pondering a moment before looking back up at me with that goofy grin he gets when he has a good comeback. "I hope you're not in a rush, because we could be here for a while." We both laugh, but I remind Dad that I want the straight goods.

"Well, Douglas, sometimes the stock market can be a difficult thing for people to understand. When it's good, it can be really good—and when it's bad, it can be downright nasty. It's volatile and unpredictable in the short term, so unless you're interested in being invested for the long haul, your chances of making money are about the same as flipping a coin. Sorry to be a bad-news bear, but that's just the way it is.

"Now," he says, slowing down a little, "if you want to talk long term, well, that's a completely different story. The odds of making money long term are very much in an investor's favour. That's why I always say that if you want to build long-term wealth, think ownership, either in the stock market, real estate or, I suppose, your own business. I happen to like the stock market.

"When you look at overall stock market risk, you have to consider both specific industry risk and individual company risk. Every company and, for that matter, every industry within the economy, has its own unique risk. For example, pity your local travel agent . . . and the whole travel industry, for that matter. They've been completely wiped out by the Internet. When I was in Tisdale, I had to do a little bit of everything to survive, so I used to make a decent buck selling airline tickets. Now those poor sods don't have a chance. How about the airline business? Fuel prices keep going up, and while ticket prices keep rising, the industry as a whole never seems to make any money. You don't need to worry about trying to find an individual airline to invest in. My advice would be stay away from the whole industry."

I feel like we're getting a bit off topic. "What about portfolio risk, Dad?" I ask. I cast my mind back to the hundreds of clients I've worked with over the years. They're the same as most investors out there—wanting to make a decent return without taking any more risk than they have to. One of my goals is to always educate them about risk and return, so I always start by explaining in basic terms how the type, quality and mix of cash, bonds and stocks determine the expected return and associated level of risk for any portfolio.

"Remember that expected returns are made up of a wide range of annual returns, some positive and some negative," Dad says. His words snap me out of my thoughts, and I start writing again. "The greater the variance of these returns, the higher the volatility and hence risk of that particular investment. Conversely, the tighter the consistency of the returns, the lower the variance and therefore the risk of that particular investment."

While we're on the topic of portfolio risk, I want to shift gears a bit and talk about industry and home country bias. This topic always elicits a lively debate between us. "Dad, let's talk about your decision to invest a large part of your portfolio in bank stocks and, while we're at it, your lack of foreign investments." He laughs and says, "I knew you'd eventually want to bring that up. I know that conventional wisdom says I'm too concentrated in bank stocks, and what international mutual funds I did have, I sold off a few years ago. Well, here's my thinking—you can invest around the world or you can invest in Canada. I agree that it's a good idea to diversify outside of Canada. I held Templeton and Trimark international funds for many years, but eventually got fed up with them because they were losing money."

I remind Dad that there were a few reasons those particular funds lost money over the first decade of the new millennium. First, investors have placed a premium on the stock of resource-oriented Canadian companies that have supplied the raw materials needed to build worldwide infrastructure over the past decade. For example, let's look at China. It's rapidly moving from an agrarian base to an industrial base and has had an insatiable appetite for our resources. The second reason for the decline in value of international mutual funds is that this natural resource boom has increased the demand for the Canadian dollar, causing it to rise from about US$0.62 in the mid to late '90s to plus or minus parity today. This change caused any US dollar–denominated investments held by Canadian investors to decline by the same amount as the rise in value of the Canadian dollar. Finally, other than the nice little run-up the US markets have had in recent months and our subsequent pause, US and world markets have underperformed our Canadian market over the last decade. The net result has been negligible returns for Canadians investing in foreign markets over this period.

In the end, individual investors have to decide what type of risk they prefer to take. There's no "one size fits all" approach. Dad takes a lot of industry and country risk by having a large component of his portfolio in the Canadian banking industry. Conversely, he takes no foreign currency risk. Personally, I prefer to have both industry and international diversification, so I take less industry and country risk and more currency risk. Who's right and who's wrong? I obviously think I'm right, but as Dad likes to say to me at times like this, "My strategy won't necessarily work for anyone else but it works just fine for me, and that's all I have to worry about."

Before we move on to specific risks associated with leveraging, I want to touch on political and tax policy risk. Some governments are elected, some are not. Some are stable, some are not. Tax policies vary widely from country to country. Canadian tax policy is relatively stable when compared with that of many other countries, but still subject to change at any time. For example, Dad's leveraging strategy relies on the fact that interest expense for investment purposes is tax deductible. It would be hard to imagine any government changing this, but as the old saying goes, "Never say never."

Since we're getting near to mid-afternoon and I've agreed to mow Dad's lawn today, I suggest that it may be a good time for him to rest up while I tackle the lawn. He readily agrees and heads to his bedroom for a nap. I step outside, get out the lawnmower and slowly start to make my way around his yard. The smell of freshly cut grass awakens my senses and opens my mind to some of the things we've been discussing today.

I review our risk discussion in my mind as I push his old-style "human" powered mower around his yard, one step at a time. I reflect on how my dad has also taken a "one step at a time" approach with his investment program. A little bit of physical activity provides a nice change of pace to an afternoon of financial talk, so I feel reinvigorated as I settle back into my deck chair, feet up, with a frosty glass of iced tea.

Forty-five minutes later, Dad reappears right on cue, ready to resume our discussion. "Did you have a good nap, Dad?" I ask. "Oh, about the usual," he responds, as he has hundreds of times to this question. As he gets older, I've observed that he has more catnaps during the day, making up for his less-restful nocturnal sleeping patterns. Some of these naps are official, when he heads for his bedroom, and some are "unofficial," when he drops off in his chair—often, it seems, when I'm in mid-sentence. Initially I felt a little slighted by this, but now I just chuckle when it happens.

The ultimate insult occurred two years ago when my late Uncle Ken and I were visiting Dad on his eighty-ninth birthday. I thought I was on a pretty good roll about the Canadian economy, but knew I was in trouble when their responses became more rote and void of any expression. Their glassy eyes were a precursor of what was coming. I lost both of them in the same sentence, heads bobbing down as they surrendered to the pleasures of a mid-afternoon siesta. Afterwards we shared a good laugh and picked up right where we had left off.

Specific leveraging risks

Dad is set to go, so I fire another question at him. "Okay, we've established that a number of risks are associated with normal stock market investing, but what are the additional risks investors should know about if they're considering leveraged investing?"

"Well, Douglas, the greatest risk all investors face is themselves. While we all want to make decisions based on logic, we need to remember that emotions and emotional management play an even greater role in investment success than logic. We're all motivated by fear and greed, so at any point in time stock markets reflect the aggregate of investor fear or greed, moving in sync with the prevailing emotion of the day.

"Now when it comes to leveraged investing, you need to understand that gains and losses are amplified. People have no problem with the gains side of the equation, but they'll struggle with the downside part. Markets increase about 70% of the time, so by logical extension, they decrease the other 30% of the time. This means that 30% of the time, leveraged investors are going to be dealing with not only the normal emotional impact of losing money, but the added impact of amplified losses. We're all wired differently, so some people handle this emotion better than others."

I'd like to ask Dad a couple of questions about his personal experience with this, but he's clearly not finished, so my questions will have to wait. "How well we manage our emotional response in negative market conditions will go a long way in determining how successful we are as stock market investors, especially as leveraged investors. I've always been able to take the long-run view of stock markets, so I tend to handle short-term volatility fairly well. Obviously, I don't like it, but I've been around long enough to see that the 70% up, 30% down rule is pretty accurate over the long term, so you just have to get through the down 30% and make sure you're there to participate in the up 70%. You either believe in these long-term numbers and stay in the game or you don't—it's really as simple as that.

"However," Dad cautions, "it's a good idea to have some sort of a plan in place, or maybe a checklist to refer back to as a reminder of how you said you were going to handle the stock market corrections that will inevitably come along. I don't want this to go to your head, Douglas, but I've been lucky to have you and John to rely on for advice during these periods."

This perks me up, and I sit up straighter. "Does this mean that you would recommend having a trusted advisor around to help you chart your course if you're thinking about leveraged investing?" I ask, somewhat suggestively.

"Yes, I suppose," Dad replies dryly, "that is, if you're able to find a good one!"

"I know at least one you can recommend," I tease back.

Dad continues: "Investors should know and understand that there is always risk when borrowing money for investment purposes. Loans need to be repaid, regardless of how well or poorly the investments associated with them do. I haven't found one banker that has a whole lot of sympathy for me or how I might be feeling during market corrections. In fact, the worse the correction, the more they are concerned with covering their own butts! In the end, they always want their money back . . . and when they come asking, there's not a lot of small talk," he says with a rueful laugh.

"And what about interest rates?" Dad asks rhetorically, as if to no one in particular. "Over my lifespan I've seen them high and I've seen them low, but never as low as they are today. Will they go up? Yes, of course they will. But remember, they'll only go up if economic activity picks up, so we should see some better stock market returns as they're rising. Let's not forget that the government picks up its share of the interest cost, since it allows me to write off this expense against my other taxable income. However, investors should never get too complacent with this write-off, as they always need to be able to cover the interest cost or risk overextending themselves."

"I couldn't agree more, Dad," I respond. As you might expect, in my line of work I've heard more than a few horror stories about people who've overextended themselves with leverage or other debt and left themselves in a vulnerable position. I can't emphasize how important it is to have sufficient liquidity and cash flow to properly fund a leverage program. This is after having sufficient cash reserves to fund life's financial emergencies, which inevitably come along, usually at the most inopportune times.

"The next thing you have to worry about is margin calls," Dad says. "Banks and brokerage houses allow you to borrow up to a predetermined credit limit based on your portfolio value and overall financial position. For example, my brokerage house has no problem matching my investment dollars. This means I'm doubling down, half of my total investment is my money and the other half is the bank's money. I wouldn't necessarily recommend this much leverage for most people, mind you. You must remember that I started out with a small amount of leverage that's grown to the present level over thirty-five years, so I've had a long time to get comfortable with it."

"Any other risks readers should know about before starting a leverage program?" I inquire.

"Yes," Dad replies, "but I should make one more comment about margin risk. Looking back, I may have taken on a little too much debt. I always allowed for a 25% market correction, which I knew would cause my portfolio to drop 50%, since I was matching my money with lender money. However, when the market corrected 35% in 2008, I got a 70% correction." I wince to show him I remember it well. Dad stops momentarily and sighs. "The positive thing is that I—we, to be more accurate—hung in there and have had a very nice comeback. But honestly, I don't know if I could emotionally survive another setback like that— you don't go through something like that without coming out the other side with a few bumps and bruises. However, you also come out a little wiser than what you were going in" he adds, with a hint of a smile.

I sometimes wonder how we ever got Dad through 2008 and early 2009. As difficult as it was, Dad's life experience puts this into proper perspective. "Listen, Douglas, I spent a winter in a granary for my Grade 12 year. Losing money is never fun, but it's nothing compared to trying to survive a minus 35 blizzard when all you've got is a few blankets, a little cookstove and four plywood walls. And we had more than a few days like that," he adds for emphasis. "Now you know why I keep my house so warm in the winter!" He laughs heartily at his admission as he knows that he keeps his house abnormally warm, especially in winter, which is totally against his frugal nature.

Leveraging and real estate

I've done my best to give you the straight goods on leveraged investing. I've given you an honest appraisal of the risks—and a taste of the possible rewards. But maybe after all this, you still may not be too sure what to think. Perhaps you're somebody who believes that borrowing to invest is "just too risky." Maybe you've been told that leveraging is only for the super-rich who can afford to gamble with their millions. Or perhaps you're questioning whether leveraged investing is suitable for small-time investors like you: normal folks who are just as concerned about protecting their precious retirement capital as they are in creating additional wealth.

I can understand your thinking but consider this: you may be leveraging right now, without even knowing it. What's more, your neighbour probably is too. In fact, I'd be willing to bet most of the people on your street are involved in the same type of risky activity. You just call it by a different name: a mortgage. That's right. If you own a home and have a mortgage, you're already in a leverage program—and have been in one for possibly a long time. If you're fortunate enough to be finally mortgage-free, then congratulations! You've already benefited immensely from the power of leveraging.

When you think about leveraged investing in these terms, it shouldn't seem quite so scary. I remember when I bought my first property. Butterflies fluttered inside my stomach as I signed my name on the dotted lines, again and again, the lawyer thrusting more and more forms at me, until finally I came to the mortgage papers. I slowed down, scanning the words carefully. I'm being diligent, I told myself, but really I was just buying time. The moment of truth came at the bottom of the page, the blank line awaiting my signature. And then, with the scratch of a pen, it was done. I was a property owner.

It was 1979—Lethbridge, Alberta. My wife at the time, Grace, and I cobbled together enough money for a down payment from savings and family, so, along with a mortgage from our local credit union, we were able to buy a nice little three-bedroom bungalow for the princely sum of $52,500. No leveraging, no mortgage, no home. It's that simple. You probably did something similar.

Why do Canadians do so well financially with their homes? The most obvious reason is pride of ownership and the fact that homeowners treat their homes as long-term investments. Consider, for example, how a mortgage amortization schedule works. With every monthly payment you pay off an ever-increasing (albeit a small amount) part of the principal. Did I hear someone say "locked-in savings plan"? Of course I did, and that's a major reason owners grow their equity in their housing investment.

Maybe another reason why we don't feel threatened by mortgages is because most people buy a house as a place to live, as a place to put down roots and make memories. Take my dad, for example. Until recently he wouldn't even consider the thought of moving out of "his" house—the same one he and Mom bought when they first moved to Lethbridge twenty-five years ago. My siblings and I had discussed the idea with him for years, but he simply didn't want to leave.

In the fall of 2012 the family got him to concede somewhat; he grudgingly agreed to have a care worker come in to look after him. Whenever I asked him why he didn't want to move, his reply was always the same: "What? Sell the house? Now you listen to me, Douglas," he'd say, shaking his finger menacingly at me, "let's get a couple of things straight. I have no desire to leave this place. This is my home. This is where I'm most comfortable. In fact, this is where I belong—it's me, it's who I am. Besides," he always added, "it's the final piece of my buy-and-hold strategy. You know, the one I've had so much success with. How could I honestly say I was being true to my investing principles if I ever sold?"

We both knew Dad used this line to get me off his back and immediately put an end to the moving talk. But as I've been writing this book, I've been thinking a lot about different ways to help explain the concepts we're covering, and I think Dad was on to something important here. In many ways, the choice to purchase a home *is* the quintessential example of "buy and hold" thinking. This thought process probably goes all the way back to his years growing up on the farm, when short-term thinking simply wasn't an option. Dad has just extended this thinking to his investment portfolio, which is exactly what you'd expect from a Prairie farm boy.

If you look carefully at Dad's investment decisions, they were made with long-term goals in mind. He has always held his investments for years, if not decades. In fact, he's only ever sold investments when he absolutely had to, as in the global economic crisis of 2008–09, when he had to sell to avoid a margin call, that dreaded call from your banker advising you that you need to pay down your loan immediately. Failing that, the banker will start selling off your portfolio to bring your margin account debt level back to within acceptable limits.

But getting him to sell anything was like pulling hens' teeth. His reluctance to sell is partly for tax reasons, for sure—but I think it is also because, just like owning a home, Dad has pride of ownership. He takes great pride in owning those iconic Canadian banks, caring about them passionately in much the same way he still cares passionately about owning his own home—much as his father cared about owning the land. Not any old land; this was the family farm, and Grandfather's whole future was staked on it. So like father, like son, I suppose.

One final note: too many people have been drawn into leveraging programs only to lose money, their hard-earned savings, because they weren't prepared for the emotional roller coaster that is a normal part of this more aggressive investing strategy. Remember, when the market rises, your gains are greater than those of a non-leveraged investor. But conversely, when the market drops, your losses are also proportionately greater than those of a non-leveraged investor.

You need to understand that you're dealing with financial rocket fuel here. Applied in the right mixture and in accordance with strict planning guidelines, leveraged investing can lead to exceptional returns. But too much leverage, placed in the wrong hands or in the wrong mixture, can also lead to disastrous results.

Educating yourself on all aspects of the strategy is the key to its successful usage—and that's what this book is all about.

Chapter 10

It's Your Money: Don't Give It Away Without a Fight

WE ARE ALL FAMILIAR WITH THE SAYING "NOTHING IN THIS WORLD CAN BE SAID TO BE CERTAIN, EXCEPT DEATH AND TAXES." You earn it—the government taxes it. You spend it—they tax it. You save it—they tax it. You invest it—they tax it. You die—and they *still* tax it! It's enough to make you think of the famous lyrics by Sting: "Every breath you take / Every move you make . . ." they'll be watching you, waiting to move tax dollars from your hands to theirs. Since you can't avoid the long outstretched arms of the Canada Revenue Agency entirely, the best you can do is to develop appropriate tax and investment strategies that will shorten its grasp—with the ultimate goal of keeping more of your money in your pocket.

My dad has never much liked the idea of paying tax. It's not that he believes the government shouldn't provide public services. It's more because he doesn't think politicians are careful enough about how they spend taxpayers' money. The way Dad sees it, he's lived his whole life trying to be as cost-efficient as possible, so he sees no reason why the government shouldn't embrace this same sensible philosophy.

Dad's views about the role of government—and the role of the state in spending taxpayer dollars—were solidified by living through the Great Depression. Prairie folk are a hardy bunch, and families like Dad's relied on themselves and their local community, not on some politician in Regina or Ottawa who claimed to care but was never there when times were tough. When you needed help, it was your neighbours in the local community you turned to, not some bureaucrat sitting at a desk in some far-off city, shuffling papers while your crops withered and died before your eyes.

I believe that this attitude of self-reliance and reciprocity that Prairie life cultivates—where you can ask your neighbour for a helping hand but not for a handout—explains why Dad has never been in favour of overcontributing to the government cookie jar. The way he sees it, he's the one who has taken the initiative, along with the associated risks, to put himself in a better financial position.

"Why should the government ride on my coattails when I do well for myself?" Dad is always quick to reply, whenever anyone probes him on the subject of taxation. "Those politicians didn't take any of the risks, so why should they share in the rewards?" In his mind, it's a reversal of fortune: he isn't relying on the government, the government is relying on him. And he's never been very happy about that.

Whenever Dad gets going on the subject of taxation, I usually let him rant for a bit, just so he feels better. Then I gently remind him that his "conscientious objector" status won't win him a reprieve from the tax department. "I know that very well, Douglas," he responds. "But it does motivate me to do all I can to reduce the amount of tax that I actually do send them. What's more, I do all I can to ensure that whatever tax I will ultimately have to pay . . ." He pauses, ponders this for a moment, then adds, "Put the emphasis on the *will* part of that statement in your book, Douglas." He wags his finger. "Maybe with some italics or something."

"Now where was I?" he says with a laugh at his momentary lapse of memory. "Yes, you tell your readers that I do everything I can to defer any tax I will ultimately have to pay." He slaps the armrest of his chair. "I know those cronies in Ottawa have designs on my money, but they better not plan on getting it any time soon, because I fully intend to use it for as long as can. And after that . . . ," his voice trails off, "well, I guess there are a few things we can't control forever."

I can't resist, so I interject: "Dad, is that the 'death and taxes' part of the equation?" Dad smiles, then replies, "Well, at least I can make them wait for it. In the meantime," he adds, "I get to use that money . . . for a greater purpose." I raise my eyebrows, and ask inquisitively, "For the greater purpose of what, Dad?" Dad doesn't miss a beat. "For the greater purpose of making a little more money for me, of course," he replies with a little chuckle.

"Douglas, I don't want your readers to think I talk the talk but don't walk the walk. So you remind them that I currently owe the government about a million dollars in deferred taxes on my unrealized capital gains. And you can quote me as saying that Ottawa won't see a cent of that until I'm six feet under." More notebook scratching on my part. Dad carries on. "By then, I hope to have earned another 10% a year on it—on money that's really theirs. It doesn't get much better than that, now, does it?"

Dad's "four kinds of dollars"

As you can see, my dad takes great pride in minimizing his taxes. This attitude has served him well over the years, and I certainly don't see it abating as he gets older. If anything, it may be getting stronger. One of the things he loves to discuss is his "four kinds of dollars," so I ask Dad if he can provide readers with a short summary of this concept. "Douglas," he replies, "there's nothing that gives me more pleasure than getting people started in the right direction when it comes to saving taxes. Can we talk about it now?" He doesn't wait for my affirmation before starting.

"The first dollar is my '61-cent dollar.' Not surprisingly, this is my least preferred dollar. I'll take it, but I sure can do a lot better elsewhere. These are the dollars we all earn from employment income, pension, RRSP and RRIF income, interest income and foreign dividends. I've named this my '61-cent dollar' because this is what we end up with here in Alberta if we're in the highest marginal tax bracket. Now you folks in B.C. get hit a little harder than we do. It appears your government needs a few extra dollars to help you all live in Lotusland, so you only get about a 56-cent dollar, if I remember correctly. And I do believe that good ol' Ontario takes even more . . . but I guess that's the price those poor sods have to pay to live in the centre of the universe," he snorts.

"Now, the second kind is my 80-cent dollar. That's the after-tax share of my capital gains that I earn on the sale of any stock I own." He pauses to give me time to write this down. "Right after that is my 81-cent dollar. It's pretty much the same as my 80-cent dollar, but as I always say, 'A penny saved is a penny earned.' That's my after-tax share of earnings from any dividends I receive from publicly traded Canadian companies." Dad knows that I know all this, but he still likes to recite it from memory. I think it helps him prove to himself that his mind is still sharp. "It's not my favourite dollar," he says, "but it sure is more likeable than the 61-cent dollar you met earlier, right?" I smile.

"Now, Douglas, I want you to meet my 98-cent dollar." He rocks his chair back and forward slowly, like he's relaxing with an old friend. "These are the dollars that I really like. In fact, even at my advanced age, they still get me cranked up. My 98-cent dollar happens when I buy a stock or piece of real estate and hold it for a long time. By holding onto my investment for many years, rather than selling it today and receiving an 80-cent dollar, I eventually grow it into a 98-cent dollar. This doesn't occur overnight . . . but remember what happens when you defer taxes to the future?" Dad doesn't wait for me to answer. "That's right," he says, "you get to use the government's money to make yourself more money."

"Remember, capital gains only occur when an investment is sold. So no sale, no capital gain, no tax. They'll eventually get their pound of flesh, but you get to control when they actually receive it. This untaxed growth that occurs over time on investments is termed an unrealized capital gain (or loss, depending on your fortunes). So, if you have the patience to hold onto your investments, before you know it you'll be saying hello to your first 98-cent dollar."

Dad pauses. He's not sure if he needs to explain this further. I raise my pen. "You'll explain the benefits of a 'buy and hold' strategy to your readers, Douglas? That if you find good, quality companies and hang on to them for the long term, there's no leakage of taxes paid to the government . . . and hence, you retain all your capital and get to use it to earn more income and growth along the way?"

"I've got it down right here, Dad," I say as I show him my notes.

"And second, make sure your readers understand that when they eventually do pay tax on these investments—whether ten, twenty or thirty years down the road—inflation will have reduced the purchasing power of the taxes you pay." Knowing that I've got his ideas down on paper allows Dad to relax a little. He leans back in his chair with his elbows on the armrests, allowing his hands to rest comfortably on his stomach. "Okay, Douglas, that wasn't an easy topic to cover," he proclaims, "but I think we've got it just about right. I know it's too early to stop for the day, but where I come from you get with the sun and work till your work is done. Some of us get up earlier than others, but that's a different issue. Now," he says, as he reaches for his glass, "let's relax with a cold drink."

The theory behind Dad's tax philosophy

After spending the previous evening leisurely working the kinks out of my golf swing at the local driving range, morning leaves me feeling refreshed and ready to face the day, another hot one even by July standards for southern Alberta. I glance through the kitchen window and catch the reading on Dad's thermometer—82 degrees. Boy, they really get the heat here, I think to myself as I swallow the last spoonful of oatmeal porridge. I also think, when the heck is Dad ever going to update that old thermometer? Canada has been using the Celsius scale since the late '70s!

"It looks like it's going to be another scorcher out there," Dad says. "The boys could sure use a little rain, but there's nothing foreseeable in the forecast." Even though Dad's been off the farm for more than seventy years, his mind is still tuned into the agricultural growing cycle, and he's always looking for news on how the crops are coming along.

We both ponder our own thoughts for a moment before I break the silence, wondering how he slept last night. "Oh, about the usual," he says. "In retrospect, we probably shouldn't have started on the whole tax thing yesterday, because it got me all revved up and I tossed and turned most of the night. I finally gave up and got up around five, and I've been waiting for you to get up ever since." He yawns deeply as if to verify his lack of sleep and says, "Anyway, son, you've got my attention now, so let's get started. I suggest we head downstairs to the nerve centre, where it's not so hot. I don't know how long I'll last before I need a nap."

Watching Dad move slowly and deliberately down the stairs reminds me that we've got to get that motorized chair system that will move him up and down the stairs installed sooner rather than later. The family suggested that we move his office upstairs, but he said it wouldn't be the same so we compromised on the stairwell transportation system and left his office downstairs. One more thing to do, I think, but the reality is that one missed step could completely change Dad's life.

Once downstairs, Dad settles comfortably into his worn but functional office chair, a green upholstered beauty—circa 1975. We used to tease him about how old it was, threatening to order a new chair online and have it delivered to his house, but he would always say, "You'll do no such thing. My chair is perfectly fine." So this classic piece of office heritage remains a fixture in his little world.

Dad asks for a few minutes to get his ideas together before we start. I can see this tax stuff really gets him going. Once he has a few thoughts down on paper, Dad starts right in. "I think the best way to introduce the whole tax subject is to first of all look at the theory behind general tax policy. Then I can explain how I operate within this framework to make sure that more money stays with me rather than getting siphoned off to you-know-who. You must remember, son, those guys have lots of high-priced accounting, tax and legal staff at their disposal to help them remove money from our pockets. So little guys like me need to be pretty sharp if we want to have any sort of a chance in the tax game."

I'm still standing, but I sense this isn't going to be a short "lecture," so I ease into the chair opposite Dad's desk. "Okay,

Douglas, the first thing you need to understand is how the tax system works. There are two types of basic taxes in Canada: income taxes and consumption taxes. On the income tax side, there are different tax rates for employment and pension (including RRIF) income, interest income, Canadian dividends and capital gains. I'll get into more detail on this in a moment. And on the consumption tax side, we've got provincial sales tax (PST), goods and service tax (GST), or in some provinces HST, which combines PST and GST. This means that all of us—in one way, shape or form—determine our level of tax participation by how we structure our working, saving, investing and consumption patterns."

I know where this is going. Dad's going to ramble on about how frugal he is. I'll let him go for a bit then rein him in, reminding him that we've already covered his "Don't live beyond your means" philosophy in an earlier chapter. "I don't consume a lot, Douglas," he says, "partly because of my age, and partly because I'm not much of a spender. We're lucky here in Alberta to not have a provincial sales tax like most other provinces—must be all the oil money, I guess, but anyway this suits me fine. My overall contribution to government revenues based on my consumption is therefore rather minimal, as I only have to worry about the GST. Now, the guys that are buying fancy cars, homes and other luxury items . . . well, those boys are getting hit hard, but they'd never take my advice to spend less anyways, so there's no point me worrying how much tax they're paying to support their 'fat cat' lifestyles."

I respond by pointing out that "those boys" are actually helping to keep the economy moving. And some of "those boys" are actually "those girls."

"I'm fine on both those points, Douglas. I don't care who the big spenders are, as long as their big tax bills don't come anywhere near me. Besides, I don't even know where I'd start if I wanted to go on a spending spree. Oh, I suppose I could head to

London or New York and start throwing some money around." He chuckles at the thought. "But I'm too old for that."

I sit upright. "Dad, I think I've already got enough material from you about these 'big spenders' and their mixed-up lifestyles," I say with a slight smile. "So let's talk about income taxes. That's the thing most readers will find the most useful, anyway."

Dad grunts. "Fine," he says. "This is pretty simple stuff." He shifts a bit in his chair, which creaks in response. "First, always try to reduce your current tax bill. Second, always try to defer your taxes to the future. That way you keep your money invested, which means it stays working for you. If your readers need a refresher on the importance of compound interest, I'm always happy to talk about that, but it might be easier for them to just go back to that section of the book," he says. I put an exclamation mark in my notebook, as a reminder to myself for future reference. "And finally, start your planning today to reduce the tax on your future income." He stops talking and rocks back in his chair. "That pretty much covers that topic, Douglas. What's next?"

"Well, now that you're on a roll, I would like to know your feelings on the role that income tax planning plays in wealth creation and how you go about minimizing your contribution to government coffers," I say. "Another favourite subject Douglas," Dad responds. "Why don't I jot a few things down on the subject while you get us a cold drink. Then I'll be ready to get into the more serious stuff, when you get back," he says.

Dad's tax philosophy in action

It's difficult to put tax planning strategies into neat little compartments so that you're either reducing current taxes, deferring taxes to the future or planning to reduce future taxes, usually in retirement. Some strategies impact only the present, while others impact both the present and the future, allowing you to save taxes today and defer taxes to the future. To use a baseball analogy, you hit a "grand slam" in tax planning with strategies that combine saving taxes today, deferring taxes to the future *and* reducing future taxes.

An example of a tax planning grand slam is Dad's leveraged buy-and-hold investment strategy, where he accomplishes all three of the tax planning possibilities:

1. The interest expense on his investments reduces current income taxes payable.

2. Since he holds his investments for the long term, he defers any unrealized capital gain taxes indefinitely to the future.

3. Because he concentrated on a leveraged investment strategy rather than an RRSP strategy, his retirement income is mainly in the form of dividends rather than RRIF income, which reduces his tax bill by about 40% when compared to taxes paid on RRIF income.

At age ninety-one, Dad's future is now. Whatever tax he's paying today is a direct result of more than three decades of tax planning. I've been fortunate to have had a "real life" tax laboratory to examine and evaluate the tax savings and the incredible tax efficiency of the retirement income he's created over this period of time.

"Thanks, Douglas," Dad says as I return with the drinks and settle back into my chair. "Where were we?" he begins. I show him the notes I've scrawled down on my pad of paper. "Hmm, I like the bit about the 'grand slam,'" he says. "I like to think of myself as a bit of a 'power' hitter in this department," he adds as we share a laugh.

Dad wastes no time getting to the main point of tax planning. "Now, Douglas, what you have to realize is that you get one kick at the can if you're serious about saving current income taxes. You can either do nothing and the government takes all your tax dollars, or you can fight back, take some action, and keep as many of those tax dollars in your pocket as you can. It's about that simple. You won't be surprised to learn that my preference is the 'taking action' route." I nod. "Yes, Dad, I kind of figured that was your preferred route." Dad doesn't sense the subtle sarcasm in my voice, but interprets my comment as a validation of where he's going with this.

"The two best ways that I can think of for ordinary Canadians to reduce their taxes," Dad continues, "is to either contribute to RRSPs or to develop a leveraging program that creates tax-deductible interest expenses. Both reduce your taxable income and current tax bill, but the leveraging approach does a much better job of reducing taxes in retirement, so it's my first choice overall. However, a combined leveraging and RRSP program is a great way for investors to have the best of both worlds. It allows you to start slowly and 'grow' into the leverage side of things while getting a good initial tax break from the RRSP. I can certainly live with that.

"Later on you can do an RRSP 'freeze,' using the RRSP to fund the interest expense of your leveraging program. This transfers future growth that would have occurred in the higher-taxed RRSP to your leverage program and the lower tax cost associated with dividends or capital gains. Everyone owes it to themselves to minimize their taxes, both today and in retirement. The most important thing is to always keep your money in your pocket," he says, patting his left hip to emphasize his point.

"I've worked the leveraging side to the point where I've paid very little taxes over the last thirty years. I would challenge anybody to do it better. I'll get out the spreadsheet and show you . . ." he leans down and starts opening his desk drawer, but I wave him off. "Let's just talk concepts right now, Dad," I say. "We'll talk actual numbers another day." Now it's Dad's turn to nod in agreement. "Alright, Douglas," he says, "but this tax differential between dividends and capital gains versus RRIF and pension income in retirement is a big deal, so I want to revisit that again. Jot it down, Douglas, so we don't forget. Something like 'Reducing retirement income tax by 40% to 50% is important.'" He pauses for a moment and then crows, "Is that a good deal or what?!"

Dad and I have been having this discussion for as long as I can remember. And after looking at these options from every conceivable angle, I have to agree with him. "You're right, Dad. Everyone should do everything they can to save taxes, and this opportunity is only available one year at a time. If you miss your chance, it's gone forever. In the case of RRSPs, you do get another chance, since you're able to defer any unused contributions to future tax years. Other than that, say *sayonara* to any current-year tax saving opportunities once you're into the last verse of 'Auld Lang Syne' and the first taste of champagne that greets a new year."

Deferring taxes to the future

I can see that Dad is starting to tire a bit, so I urge him on. "Okay, Dad, let's talk about your strategy of deferring taxes." As I say this I fold over the page of my notepad and write DEFERRING TAXES TO THE FUTURE at the top of the next page. "I'll bet you've got a few things to say about that." Dad snaps back, "Indeed I do, Douglas. So, once you've done everything you can to reduce your current tax bill, the next thing you need to think about is how you're going to start deferring every tax dollar you can into the future. Remember our discussion about the power of compounding? Well, deferring taxes to the future leaves you with a larger capital base to create more future growth for your portfolio. Nothing much happens in the first few years," he says, "but over a lifetime, the difference is huge. For example, RRSPs and unrealized gains in regular or leveraged accounts are prime examples of capital bases that are growing on a tax-deferred basis. I hate to keep harping on about it, but I get to use the future cost of my deferred tax bill on my unrealized gains to make me more money right now because my capital base is retained. And I like that. In fact, I like that a lot!

"Furthermore, Douglas, whatever income I actually need for my retirement can come out in the form of dividends and/or capital gains at between 50 and 60% of the tax cost of interest income, pension, RRSP or RRIF income. It's not that these other types of income are bad. It's just that dividend income and capital gains are so much more tax-efficient. Since we retired people no longer have employment income to support us, we need to stretch our dollars as far as we can." Dad pauses. "An important part of this process is to minimize the dollars we pay out to our 'friends' in Ottawa. This helps to ensure that we have enough money to be comfortable in our 'golden' years, whatever the hell that means."

Dad continues: "Well, I think I've already let 'the cat out of the bag,' or as we on the Prairies like to say, 'the bull out of the barn' a couple of times, as I can't seem to keep a good thing quiet, but the final thing you need to do in the tax planning game is to minimize your taxes payable in your retirement years. There's no point wasting a lifetime of great tax planning by giving it all away to the government once you're retired."

It appears that Dad has at least one more point to make. "Unfortunately, your options to reduce your tax bill in retirement become somewhat limited if you haven't been planning for it all along. You have to start taking income out of your RRSP when you turn seventy-two. While it's always a good thing to receive extra income in retirement, it's also a lottery for the tax department, which receives up to 40% of that income (in Alberta). That's a negative. However, I've countered that with my leverage program. I currently owe the government about $1 million of tax on the unrealized gains present in my portfolio—but remember, I get to decide when to sell my investments and pay that debt. I like the fact that I control that decision. In the meantime, I get to use that money to make more money . . . and you can probably guess how I feel about that," he says, with a sparkle in his eyes.

"I think we better wrap things up here, Douglas. I don't want to sound like a skipping record here, but damn it, you get me all wound up and then I can't seem to stop. Oh well," he adds with a sigh, "as long as your readers feel the same way I do, this will all be worthwhile. First they need the facts, but eventually they need to take action. Maybe if we all start keeping more of our money in our own pockets instead of sending it to Ottawa, the politicians and their high-priced bureaucrats will get the message and start spending within their means . . . just like the rest of us. And you can quote me on that one, Douglas."

"I just did," I respond. "It's going in the book." He slaps me on the back. "Come on, son, let's get another drink. You're working your old man pretty hard these days." Before we head upstairs I caution Dad that the heavy lifting is just beginning, as I want to review his investment story from day one to the present tomorrow. "In that case let's make that two cold drinks," he adds with a chuckle.

Chapter 11

Dad's Thirty-Five-Year Investment Journey

DAD'S KNOWLEDGE OF MATHEMATICS WAS HIS BIGGEST ASSET WHEN HE STARTED INVESTING. He knew enough about compound interest and taxation to understand that the ideal situation would be to have as much of his money invested as he could afford—plus a little bit more, of course. That may not be a surprising revelation (it's always better to have more money), but in my dad's case, it turned out to be a very powerful one. That's why the first thing Dad did before he invested his $200,000 was to get the banker's approval to lend him another $18,000. He understood his own money would only go so far. That's why he started leveraging.

"Douglas?" Dad obviously didn't notice that I had dozed off in my favourite chair on the back porch. He startles me somewhat so I try to pull myself together before responding. I look down and see that the ice cubes in my glass have melted. Another hot one coming, I say to myself, as I wipe a few beads of sweat from my forehead with my shirtsleeve.

"Yes, Dad?" I reply. I've been trying not to overwork him. For the last three days we've been doing very little except talk about leveraging and eat sandwiches: a tuna with mayonnaise for him and a turkey and tomato for me. But what a productive three days it's been. I'm amassing so much material I'm not sure what to do with all of it, so I've been spending each evening after Dad has gone to bed making sure everything we've talked about is down on paper.

I worked so late last night that I actually had a pizza delivered to the house so I wouldn't have to stop writing. I don't remember what time it was, but being surrounded by pizza and a bunch of papers certainly brought back old memories. I hadn't done anything like this since pulling all-nighters back at university—what a rush to be this excited about something again!

"Douglas?" Dad calls to me again, thinking I didn't hear him. When I turn my head and he sees I'm listening, he says: "Son, I think you need a day off." I pause for a second while I lift myself up in my chair.

"What'd you say, Dad?" I reply, a little taken aback. "I need a day off? From what?" Dad sniffs in a quick breath and smiles slightly. "From this whole 'book thing,' that's what! It's obviously wearing you down. You look tired, son."

I laugh to myself. Here I am, worried about overworking him—and it turns out he has the same concerns about me. "All I have to do is talk," he says. "You, on the other hand, have to make sure it all gets recorded—correctly, mind you." He exhales. "That's a lot of responsibility—and all this is over and above your day job. Sometimes I don't know how you keep it all together."

I shake my head as if to brush off his comment. "You think I'm overworked," I begin, "trying single-handedly to write up your life story, analyzing your three decades of leveraging experience, not to mention all the lessons that need to be included in this book? You think it's too much for me?" While I'm being somewhat facetious, as the words come out of my mouth I realize how much work it's actually been.

"No, that's not it, Douglas," he says. "I think you are perfectly capable of writing this book. But I couldn't help but notice the pizza box that was left on my countertop when I woke up this morning. And a pizza box," he says, "is the sign of a man who worked late into the night."

I grin sheepishly, knowing Dad has me on this one. I had promised myself I'd throw out the pizza box before Dad got up, but I guess I got distracted. "Okay, Dad, you're right. Sometimes I do feel this whole project is almost too much for me. But we can't stop now. We've got too much to do. Besides, it feels like we're really on a roll."

Dad finishes the last gulp of his lemonade. "Well, why don't we get out of the realm of abstraction and back down to earth? You said you wanted to have a section where we went through the history of my whole program from start finish. Why don't we zero in on that today? Surely that won't be too taxing." I smile at his joke, but also in appreciation of the fact that I can just sit back, listen, take notes and ask a few questions from time to time.

Dad's entry into leveraged investing

"The first thing you need to know," Dad begins, "is that back in 1978 I had no idea that I'd be dealing with the kind of numbers we're talking about today. Not even on my radar. In Tisdale I had a good real estate portfolio, with two commercial buildings and two rental properties totalling seven suites. They were all good investments, for sure, but I was getting tired of dealing with tenant problems and blocked toilets. One thing I wasn't getting tired of, however, were the tax advantages that borrowing for real estate offered. For me, investing in the stock market was really just an extension of this earlier experience in real estate. Same principle, different investment."

I scribble a few notes. "As I think back, I may have been at a point in my life where I was just looking for something different," Dad adds, pausing for a moment to reflect. "Who knows, maybe a little excitement? So I thought I'd see if I could make a little money in the market, much the same way as I did in real estate."

"Well, Dad, it sure worked," I tease, but he waves me off dismissively. "Let's be honest here, Douglas, the early years were a pretty steep learning curve." He continues, "The truth of the matter is that I may have been in a little over my head." I feign a surprised look to goad Dad on a bit, but he ignores my antics and carries on. "My lack of investment experience created a few challenges, and my investment strategy was basically of the 'hit and miss' variety." He waits for me to make some kind of a comment about this, but I resist the urge and just nod.

"I learned a lot of expensive lessons in the early years," Dad says, "but, hey, I survived the recession of '81–82. There were a lot of people who didn't, you know." I click my tongue in agreement. "A lot of people went bankrupt, lost everything. Those were the dark days of 22% interest rates and runaway inflation, resulting in big foreclosures. Everyone was worried sick," he breathes in, "but I stuck it out."

"And you were duly rewarded for that patient, long-term view," I reply, "just like a good farmer." He laughs at this.

"The mid-'80s were excellent years in the market," Dad says, "so just after my sixty-fifth birthday I decided it was time to sell my insurance agency and take things a little easier. I had been going non-stop for more than forty years and felt comfortable with a net investment portfolio of $800,000 and another $200,000 in RRSPs. My thought was to just putter around selling a few GICs and mutual funds to family, friends and a small group of clients." He shifts in his chair.

"Are you getting tired, Dad?" I ask. He chuckles before responding. "I know we're right in the middle of our conversation, but yes, Douglas, I'm feeling a wave of sleepiness coming over me. If I don't stop now and head for my bedroom, I'll be slumped over in my chair in no time flat. I used to try to fight it," he admits, "but now I just let go. I don't have anything that's too pressing these days, you know," he says with a laugh. "And Douglas, with the shape you're in after working half the night, you may want to catch a little shut-eye yourself."

I mutter something as he shuffles off. But instead of sleeping I sit quietly—pondering what Dad has just told me. He's basically saying that the whole leveraging thing wasn't about the money. For him it's always been about basics and getting things right. Do your homework, don't take shortcuts, that type of thing. Be prepared to test out new ideas, concepts and methodologies. Once you're satisfied with what you've got, you stick with it, only tweaking your strategy when new information comes along that simply cannot be ignored. "No need to reinvent the wheel," he always says.

Having said all this, we need to get one thing straight. Although this may seem like it's just a game for my dad, something to occupy his time, he takes the game seriously and plays to win. And yes, he does enjoy the "spoils" that come along with a winning performance, just as any professional athlete would.

It's this mix of the theoretical and the real that I find so fascinating about my dad's investment journey. In sports, they would say he had developed and executed an excellent "game plan." Back on the farm, it was a little more basic than that—they would say he had survived another year.

Dad's first year of retirement

Late in 1986, Dad was learning the nuances of a new word: retirement. He likes to say he was "semi-retired" (whatever that means), but in reality he was just hanging around his old office in Claresholm. Truth was, he really didn't have any plans for retirement. Like many men of his generation, Dad's life revolved around his work, so when it came time to actually retire, he wasn't well prepared.

He found his focus pretty soon, however. In a case of "be careful what you wish for," Dad woke up one Monday to a lot more excitement than he ever could have imagined. That particular Monday was October 19, 1987: Black Monday. Wall Street crashed and took world markets down with it. Dad's portfolio was not spared the carnage. When he tallied up his losses at the end of the day, it wasn't pretty—he was down a staggering $342,000, roughly a third of his net portfolio. Welcome to the real world of leveraged investing, Dad! The amplified leverage gains of the mid-'80s were now replaced by amplified leverage losses—which all came in one day.

Many investors never recovered from Black Monday. Dad might have been one of them had he let panic and fear take hold, but he didn't. Instead of dumping stocks in a desperate attempt to solve a very difficult market situation, he stuck to his principles and hung on, just like his parents had done nearly half a century earlier. He clung fast to the belief that this down period wouldn't last forever.

In the days that followed October 19th, the market was erratic, randomly moving in both directions for no apparent reason. This created significant opportunity for long-term, value-oriented investors. Sensing this, Dad did some selective buying at what would eventually prove to be bargain prices.

When the curtain finally fell on 1987, Dad showed a profit of $38,000, an excellent result in an exceptionally difficult year.

The next year, 1988, was a year of consolidation, but in 1989 Dad made $265,000 or 31% and ended the decade with a portfolio value of $1,107,000, a gain of $882,000 on his January 1, 1980, valuation of $225,000. He had regained everything he had lost in those dark days of October—and much more. Dad's patience and persistence paid off, just as it had in the 1981–82 market correction. His portfolio had increased by almost $300,000—more than a third!—in the three years since he'd retired. At this point, Dad held a combination of stocks and mutual funds, with about 70% of his portfolio in Canadian bank stocks. His largest individual holding was Templeton Growth Fund.

Dad has always been attracted to bank stocks. It's easy to see why. There's no real mystery to what banks do. The business model is straightforward: they lend money to people who want to borrow and hold money for people who want to save, earning a healthy spread between the two. Of course, today's banks are much more diversified than this, moving into new markets such as brokerage and wealth management, but deposit taking and lending are still their bread and butter. Canadian banks and indeed the Canadian banking system are both recognized worldwide for their strength in balancing the needs of depositors, the banks themselves and government monetary policy. Within the investment community, our banks have a reputation as solid investments that pay out a strong, growing dividend stream. It's this dividend stream that Dad has relied on all these years to pay the interest costs on his investment loan.

The 1990s started slowly for Dad. He was rudely introduced to the new decade with the Royal Trust bankruptcy. "That was a bad one," Dad recollects. "Royal Trust was the biggest trust company in Canada. They paid a good dividend. The stock price went down so I bought more. I kept on believing that it would turn around, but all it did was go down. I finally gave up, having lost $216,000. The Royal Bank swooped in and picked up their assets and a very knowledgeable staff for pennies on the dollar. That one really hurt."

The loss was significant because it wiped out more than 20% of Dad's portfolio. Perhaps more important than the financial loss was the psychological loss, which severely challenged his faith in the capital markets. How could something like this happen to such a large, well-respected Canadian financial institution?

By the mid-'90s, Dad's investment philosophy really started to solidify. "I had been in the game long enough to know what I liked and what I didn't like. I was investing more and more in Canadian banks, since I really liked the dividends they were paying, and using foreign mutual funds to diversify outside of Canada," Dad says. "I was down to four Canadian bank stocks, which represented about 50% of my holdings, and Templeton and Trimark mutual funds, which were another 35%."

Nineteen-ninety-six was a watershed year for my dad for a couple of reasons—his net portfolio attained a $2-million valuation for the first time ever (a tenfold increase over his initial investment in 1978, and two and a half times what he retired with in 1987), and his debt level passed though the $1-million mark for the first time ever. All this just in time for his seventy-fifth birthday in November of that year.

At Dad's birthday party, my brother John presented Dad with a personalized birthday gift: a spreadsheet. It tracked all of his individual stocks, graphing their purchasing history. But it also was prescriptive: it examined a series of what-if scenarios, and—perhaps more importantly—it projected where Dad's portfolio and debt levels should be on a monthly and annual basis.

The spreadsheet changed everything. Until that day, Dad had taken a somewhat ad-lib approach towards managing his stock holdings. His buying patterns had been fairly random, centring more on his credit availability than anything else. This resulted in him doing most of his buying when his portfolio had its greatest value and also, of course, when stock prices were at their highest levels.

The spreadsheet helped Dad realize that a more consistent dollar cost averaging purchasing strategy would help him average down his buying costs. This realization—and the resulting change in strategy—resulted in better margin account efficiency and better matching of his dividend income and interest costs, which reduced his income taxes to almost nothing. Dad's strict adherence to the spreadsheet—and his constant consultation of it—led the family to start referring to it as Dad's "bible." I remember joking with John that he might as well have chiseled that spreadsheet into two stone tablets and brought them down from a mountain peak, much like Moses had done with the Ten Commandments.

Dad had entered the 1990s with net assets of $1.1 million. He closed the decade and the millennium with net holdings of $2.4 million, a $1.9-million gain (480%) after accounting for the $600,000 he gifted to his children over that period. A significant change from the granary lifestyle of the late 1930s, I'd say.

The tech stock boom of the late '90s

The years leading up to the new millennium brought with them a new investor phenomenon: the tech stock. Computer-driven innovations drove the dot-com craze, sending stock prices for many related companies through the roof. As stock prices spiked upwards, investors jumped aboard in droves, even though most understood little about this "virtual" industry and even less about fundamental company valuation. All they saw was "the next big thing"—and they wanted a piece of the action.

Meanwhile, a new practice was emerging on the market floors around the world: day trading. The age of stock market computerization had arrived, completely transforming information flow and trade execution for a whole new generation of market traders and individual investors. Market participants could now take advantage of extremely low commission rates to maximize their trading volumes, leading to millions of lightning-speed transactions each and every day. Suddenly people were hauling in 400% gains between breakfast and lunch, or so the buzz went. A frenzy of speculation ensued, nearly doubling the technology-driven NASDAQ in less than three years.

In hindsight, it's easy to say that mixing day trading with volatile tech stocks was a recipe for disaster. But those heady years sucked a lot of people in—many who shouldn't have been there in the first place. By 2001, the tech bubble had burst, taking the NASDAQ down with it, now lower than where it had begun its stratospheric flight just three years earlier. Problem was, a lot of investors weren't prepared to end up with less than they started with. They had bet on a rosy future—and lost, big time.

Fortunately, Dad had invested the grand sum of zero dollars in the tech sector during those years. I say fortunately, but given what you've read about my dad and his outlook, that's not really surprising, is it? A long-term thinker with a buy-and-hold philosophy and a limited knowledge of this whole new "tech" thing doesn't sound like an ideal investor for this rough-and-tumble type of investing. That being said, I'm sure the allure of supposedly "easy" money must have been tempting, even for a guy like him.

I remember a conversation I had with him at the time. He wondered aloud if he—"a cautious, patient Prairie boy," as he always liked to say—was possibly being left behind. For more than a decade, his slow-growth, rock-solid bank stocks had provided him with a steady dividend stream—nothing fancy, but a good, honest cash flow. However, they were looking rather quaint and staid beside the double- and triple-digit growth the tech stocks were posting . . . or so the story went.

Being Dad's son, at first I'd always offer words of support for his position: "You're doing all the right things, Dad. Don't get caught up in all the market hype. Just stick to what you know and what you've got." But after a few big price spikes, I couldn't help but tempt him, just a bit.

"Hey, Dad," I said offhandedly, during one of our phone conversations. "You've been watching that TDZ price spike, right?" TDZ didn't even exist; I'd just invented some technical-sounding acronym. "Up more than 40% in the last forty-eight hours and they say that's just a start. I'm thinking now's the time to hop on board." I left some space, then added: "I'm pondering taking a position this week. You interested?"

If I had been face to face with Dad, this ploy would have flopped. The smile on my face would have been a dead giveaway. Besides, I didn't even have a brokerage account. But over the phone I figured maybe I had a chance at bluffing him. I wanted to see what it would take to tempt this cautious Prairie boy to take a stab at those tantalizing profits.

"You could trade some of your Scotia stock—you know, with its miserly 3% dividend—and buy TDZ straight up," I added. "I'm probably in for $5,000. A man of your stature should be in for a lot more than that. Besides, it might add a little zip and excitement to your portfolio." I was grinning ear to ear by now, but I held my voice steady, trying to keep the ruse intact.

Dad paused—a bit longer than I expected, to be honest. Then he replied: "You know me, Douglas. And that's just not me. I'm my father's son, raised on a farm, with roots firmly entrenched in the land. This tech thing might as well be from another planet," he snorted. "Where I grew up, if you felt like you were losing sight of what's really important, the true meaning of it all, you went outside and picked up a handful of dirt and let it run through your fingers. That brought you back to reality pretty fast.

"People keep talking about how there's a 'virtual' world out there now," he went on, "one where the basic realities of supply and demand don't seem to apply. A world where a bunch of computer code can make people rich faster than a Saskatchewan lightning strike. I must admit, some days I'm tempted to jump on board this whole 'tech thing,' but it's just not my game, son. I'm a patient guy who's always been in it for the long haul. To be honest, we seem to be in a short-term, flip-it fantasyland. Who knows, maybe I'm wrong, but I just don't see how it's going to last."

That's my dad. Willing to forgo the possibility of a "get-rich-quick" scheme because it didn't fit his life philosophy, let alone his investor profile. He's a guy who believes that hard work and discipline should be rewarded—not speculation in the stock market. He isn't interested in "the next big thing" if it isn't something built to last. When all was said and done, investing in tech stocks went against everything Dad believed in, and he wisely stayed away.

The new millennium

September 11th, 2001. A calm, blue-sky morning in New York City, suddenly shattered. As the world watched in horror, airplanes morphed into missiles that pierced the twin towers of the World Trade Center. Wall Street shut down for four days, creating market panic and sending global markets reeling.

World markets took their time digesting what the future might look like. They traded down to flat over the ensuing fifteen months, leaving US markets with a zero rate of return for the five-year period ending December 31, 2002. The TSX fared a little better over the same period, returning 6%, while Dad rode out the market turmoil en route to an impressive 21% return.

The years 2003 through 2007 were exceptional growth years for Dad. His portfolio benefited from above-average returns, declining borrowing costs, reduced income taxes and, of course, the continual refinement of his leverage strategy. During this five-year period, his portfolio increased from $3.2 million to $8.9—a gain of nearly $6.7 million, after accounting for nearly $1 million he gifted to his children.

Stop to think about this for a moment. Dad figures that he made about $1 million over a forty-year working career, yet using his leveraged investing strategy he made more than six times this amount in just five years. By any standards, this is remarkable.

Of course, Dad is the first to admit the markets treated him well during that period. But he also points out that he wasn't in the game just to make a quick buck. That $6.7 million didn't come from flipping stocks or speculating on futures. It came from a very deliberate strategy that combined disciplined buying decisions—he has always favoured purchasing stable, dividend-paying stock on a dollar cost averaging basis—and aggressive tax planning, where he minimized current taxes by roughly matching interest expense with dividend income and deferred capital gains tax to the future with a "buy and hold" investment strategy. This allowed him to retain all his capital and earn additional returns, even on the deferred tax he would eventually pay on his unrealized capital gains. Nothing fancy, but very, very effective.

By the summer of 2008, storm clouds were starting to appear on the horizon. The US housing market was starting to look a little "frothy," but nothing too severe, suggested the analysts. By September a commercial credit crisis halted interbank credit movement: a worrying development, but nothing we can't handle, officials assured nervous investors. Then the FOR SALE signs hanging in front of homes in Arizona, Nevada and Florida began to be replaced by FORECLOSURE notices posted on the front doors. This was the first time many of us learned about a uniquely American creation called the "subprime mortgage" and all the problems associated with this type of debt financing. Did I hear "inappropriate lending practices"? Before long, homeowners began to default on their payments or, worse yet, walk away from their homes.

The origin of the crisis was simple: government policy and opportunistic lending agencies allowed unqualified buyers to get in over their heads. When the "teaser" low interest rates expired, replaced by much higher rates, people began defaulting. Home values plummeted, often to less than the value of outstanding mortgages. As the crisis spread, more and more homeowners were finding their homes worth less and less. Soon it wasn't just the unemployed or evicted homeowners desperately trying to stay afloat. Everyone was reaching for something to hold onto. But nothing seemed to float.

Stock markets mirror the general state of the economy, and the economy didn't look good. By the end of 2008, the S&P 500 index had fallen 37%, while the TSX 300 in Canada dropped 35%. Dad was hit harder than most, since his leveraged portfolio amplified the market losses, driving his portfolio down 67%.

His world along with his portfolio hit rock bottom on March 9, 2009. Dad called me that morning, just like he had most mornings over the previous few months. I remember that call like it was yesterday—the fear in my eighty-seven-year-old father's voice, the raw emotion of a man searching for some reason in a world without reason, a man who was near the end, ready to give up.

In the midst of that telephone call, I asked Dad what he thought his father would have done. His answer was snappy: "He would have stayed the course." I asked Dad if he still believed in that strategy for his investment portfolio. He sighed deeply and said quietly, "I just don't know, Douglas. I don't know anymore."

I'm not sure why, but at that moment my thoughts turned to my grandfather. I imagined him staring out his farm window, the wind howling outside, the sky dark with dust, watching his world fall apart. And I remembered what Dad had told me about Mr. Molstad, the man from the land company who had visited my grandparents at their farm, some seventy-five years earlier.

"Hey, Dad?" I asked, breaking the silence. "What was it that Mr. Molstad said to Grandpa about the mortage payments on the farm?" No answer. I waited for what seemed like a eternity. Then Dad's voice came through.

"He said to hold on," Dad replied. "He promised my parents that nothing bad could last forever." He coughed a couple of times, then cleared his throat. "He said that even if my parents had to sell off half—no, make that most—of their land to survive, that they should never give up that last little bit. That they should always hold out hope that next year would be better."

"Okay, Dad," I replied. "Then you already know what we have to do. We need to sell some of your stocks. But you're not bowing out. We both agree on that. So hang on, Dad. There's still work to be done and you're going to make it through."

I suddenly felt strong. Dad wasn't caving in. Things were going to work out—even though I had nothing to go on but hope. But then again, that's all my grandfather had, so many years ago.

"We'll get through this," I said. "And we'll just have to hope that next year will be better."

"Okay, Douglas," Dad said. "You're right." He sighed. "So let's get started."

Over the next few days, John and I convinced Dad to sell about 20% of the stocks in his portfolio. Some were holdings he had owned for more than twenty-five years. A few, like TD and Royal Bank, were long-time favourites, and he only let them go after putting up a fight. Others, like Scotiabank and CIBC, he outright refused to sell, saying that he wasn't going to "give them away" and then pay a whopping tax bill on his accumulated gains on top of this. "No sir," he said. "I'll go along with you boys on a few of your calls, but I'll go down with the ship before I agree to everything you want me to do." In the end, he did what he had to do to survive. And, just like his father before him, he held out hope that next year would be better. And you know what? It was.

The year 2009 turned out to be Dad's best year ever. Skillful buying shortly after the market bottom in March of that year allowed Dad to replenish his portfolio at some of the same "give-away" prices he had refused to sell at. After giving $100,000 to his children, he made an amazing $2.3 million on his net opening balance of $2.7 million to close out the year at just over $5 million, a gain of roughly 85%.

When you consider that Dad gave almost $1.4 million of his $2.4 million opening 2000 balance to his children over the first decade of the new millennium, he really took the remaining balance of $1 million to $5 million over the ten-year period. Very impressive indeed, especially when you consider the volatility of markets during this period and the amplified loss associated with his leveraging strategy in 2008–09, the most debilitating stock market correction since the Great Depression.

As we closed out 2012, Dad's net portfolio was worth just over $6.6 million, a gain of $970,000 or 15% for the year and about $1.45 million or 28% for the first three years of the current decade. The key theme that one observes through the years is Dad's consistent strategy. Good years, bad years, he just quietly keeps going about his business, trying to earn a steady 10% return in a world that's anything but steady. Whenever I talk to Dad, I usually ask him how he's doing. He has a few responses but I have one that I like the best: "I'm fine, it's just the world around me that's all messed up." Touché, Dad, touché.

Chapter 12

The Numbers Tell
the Story

WHEN YOU DRILL DOWN TO THE FOUNDATION OF MY DAD'S WEALTH CREATION STRATEGY, IT'S EMBARRASSINGLY SIMPLE. I've given you a lot of information, concepts and personal stories. The time has come to give you, as the legendary Paul Harvey would say, "the rest of the story"—Dad's actual results and specific strategies used to get these results. Hopefully you can use some of these same strategies in your own retirement planning. After all, Dad wouldn't be impressed if you bought the book and got a bunch of theory with no practical applications to help you. "You'd better give your readers value for their money, Douglas," he warned me. "After all, you said you would, so you better deliver on that promise."

Okay, Dad, let's do it. Let's cut to the chase. Let's give them some real numbers, some meaty stuff they can chew on— you know, show them the money—and I mean that literally. It's time to pull out some charts that chronicle Dad's thirty-five-year investment story much better than I could ever tell it.

If you're a numbers person, you're going to love the first chart (Figure 1). If you're like most people and prefer visuals, skip over this chart as the same information is shown in graph format throughout the balance of the chapter. Okay? So here are the cold, hard numbers, not dressed up in any way. Figure 1 shows gross and net investment portfolio numbers, debt outstanding and margin ratios along with annual returns in numeric and percentage terms.

Figure 1. Dad's investment history, 1978–2012

Year	Gross Investment ($000's)	Debt Outstanding ($000's)	Amounts Redeemed ($000's)	Net Investment ($000's)	Margin Ratio (%)	One-Year Portfolio Gain ($000's)	One-Year Return (%)
1978	227	18		209	7.9		
1979	280	55		225	19.6	16	7.7
1980	425	90		335	21.2	110	48.9
1981	440	154		286	35.0	−49	−14.6
1982	403	137		266	34.0	−20	−7.0
1983	475	165		310	34.7	44	16.5
1984	691	246		445	35.6	135	43.5
1985	1,075	365		710	34.0	265	59.6
1986	1,295	482		813	37.2	103	14.5
1987	1,428	577		851	40.4	38	4.7
1988	1,283	425		858	33.1	7	0.8
1989	1,753	646	16	1,107	36.9	265	31.2
1990	1,375	573	60	802	41.7	−245	−22.7
1991	1,638	529	60	1,109	32.3	367	47.5

Figure 1. Dad's investment history, 1978–2012 (cont.)

Year	Gross Investment ($000's)	Debt Outstanding ($000's)	Amounts Redeemed ($000's)	Net Investment ($000's)	Margin Ratio (%)	One-Year Portfolio Gain ($000's)	One-Year Return (%)
1992	1,643	621	60	1,022	37.8	−27	−2.5
1993	1,675	337	60	1,338	20.1	376	37.9
1994	1,861	577	60	1,284	31.0	6	0.5
1995	2,102	525	75	1,577	25.0	368	29.5
1996	2,874	760	50	2,114	26.4	587	37.8
1997	3,865	1,028	100	2,837	26.6	823	39.9
1998	3,288	901	100	2,387	27.4	−350	−12.6
1999	3,733	1,299	—	2,434	34.8	47	2.0
2000	4,690	1,473	—	3,217	31.4	783	32.2
2001	6,045	2,501	100	3,544	41.4	427	13.5
2002	5,997	2,775	—	3,222	46.3	−322	−9.1
2003	8,215	3,634	75	4,581	44.2	1,434	45.0
2004	11,154	5,543	100	5,611	49.7	1,130	24.9
2005	15,155	7,587	150	7,568	50.1	2,107	38.1
2006	18,953	9,014	300	9,939	47.6	2,671	36.0
2007	19,324	10,382	320	8,942	53.7	−677	−6.9
2008	4,854	2,057	225	2,797	42.4	−5,920	−67.0
2009	8,680	3,638	100	5,042	41.9	2,345	85.4
2010	9,583	3,427	—	6,156	35.8	1,114	22.1
2011	8,452	2,818	—	5,634	33.3	−522	−8.5
2012	9,299	2,649	—	6,650	28.5	1,016	18.0

Still with me? Don't worry if you're not. No more numbers. Figure 2 shows you Dad's gross investment portfolio and the debt outstanding in graphic format. Notice how the debt outstanding takes the same shape as the gross investment portfolio except after 2009, when Dad started paying down his debt.

Figure 2. Gross investment portfolio & debt outstanding, 1978–2012

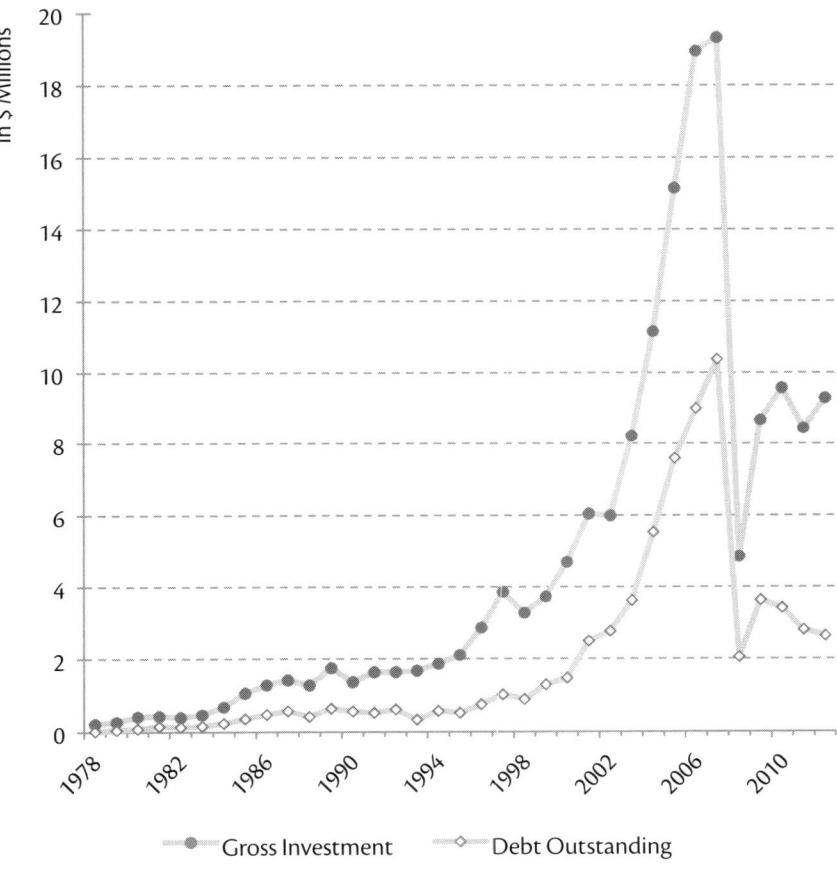

This is a beautiful chart until 2008. Down but not out, Dad stayed with his program and has made steady progress ever since. He's seen enough difficult markets to know that the best way to get through them is to stay the course.

Figure 3 shows Dad's year-by-year net investment portfolio growth over the thirty-five years, starting with $200,000 in 1978 and ending with $6.6 million in 2012—still an impressive

Figure 3. Net investment portfolio growth, 1978–2012

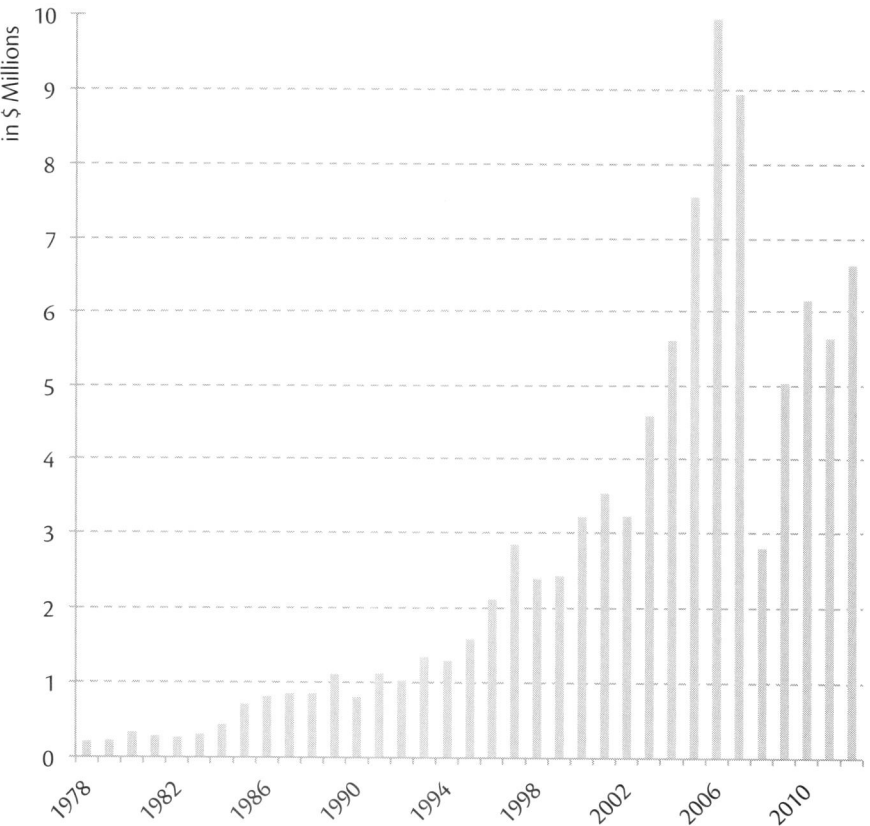

graph, even with the problems encountered by all investors in 2008. This shows the critical importance of having a long-term perspective and persevering through difficult market conditions.

Figures 4, 5 and 6 show Dad's annual return and compound five- and ten-year returns. Notice how time tends to smooth out returns. The five-year graph shows less variability than the one-year graph, and the ten-year graph shows less variability than the five-year graph (i.e., investment returns tend to be less predictable in the short run and more predictable in the long run). For this reason leveraged investing should only be considered as a long-term strategy. It's an absolute no-no in the short run.

Portfolio management

"Shut that damn thing off," Dad says to me. It's mid-afternoon, and the business channel BNN has been running on the television most of the day. I fumble around with the remote and turn the TV off. "Thank you, Douglas. I have trouble concentrating if I've got too many things going on around me," Dad explains. He pauses for a moment and then says, "You know, Marty and Frances are good commentators, but I still miss Jim, the original anchor. Poor soul died of cancer—couldn't have been much over fifty." Dad shakes his head and goes silent for a moment before adding, "It's a pretty cruel world out there, Douglas, when you see good men like that go down so early." He pauses again before carrying on. "Now, son, what was it you said you wanted to talk about today?" I mention that I want to talk about his portfolio management philosophy and how he manages everything on a day-to-day basis. We chat for a few minutes about generalities and then Dad gets more specific.

"Well, Douglas, the first thing you need to understand is what kind of investor you are. For example, I've never been much of a trader. Doesn't fit my personality. How would I compete with those talented young Bay Street and Wall Street traders? I don't have a hope in hell of matching their skills, and I wouldn't know what to do with the high-tech gadgets and data streams they all use. I learned a long time ago to play the game I know and not try to be someone I'm not. So the best I can do is to stay with what I do well. And that's being patient and thinking long

Figure 4. One-year investment returns, 1978–2012 (%)

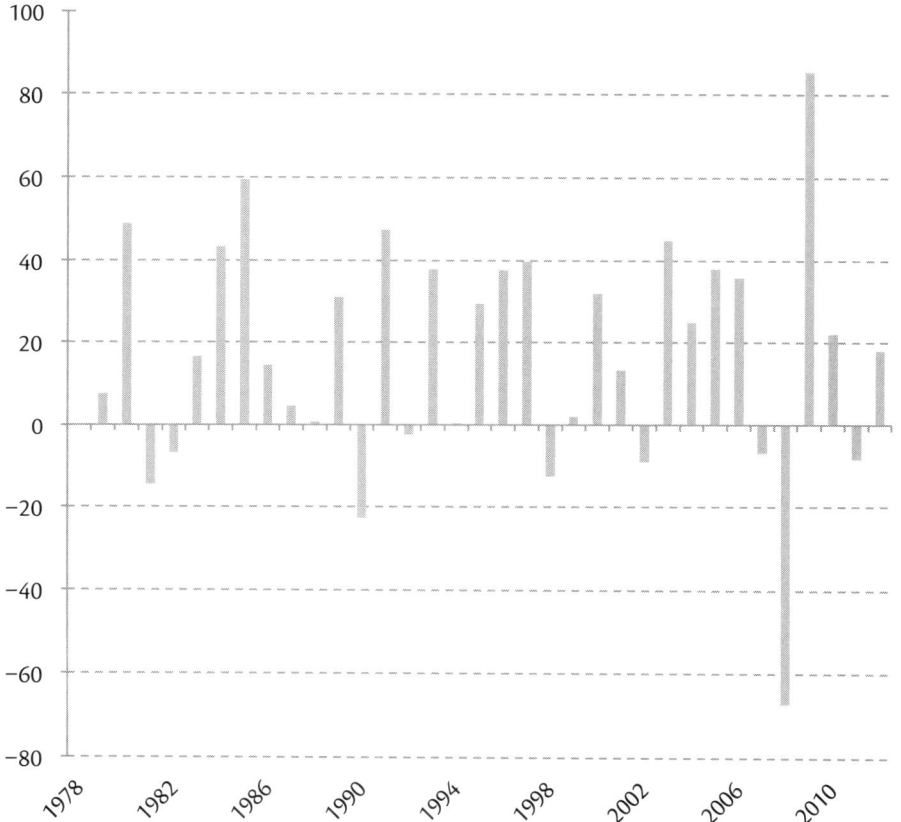

term—traits those young bucks probably think are outdated. But hey, let's check back with them in thirty-five years and see if they match my results," he says with a laugh.

"Personally, I like banks. Quality businesses—a little high on some of their customer fees, but that's okay for shareholders like me. I don't stay awake at night worrying about them. Besides, they've had a long history of paying out a growing dividend stream. Why would I start selling companies I'm perfectly happy with? Listen, Douglas, these banks and their expensive real estate

Figure 5. Five-year compound investment returns, 1983–2012 (%)

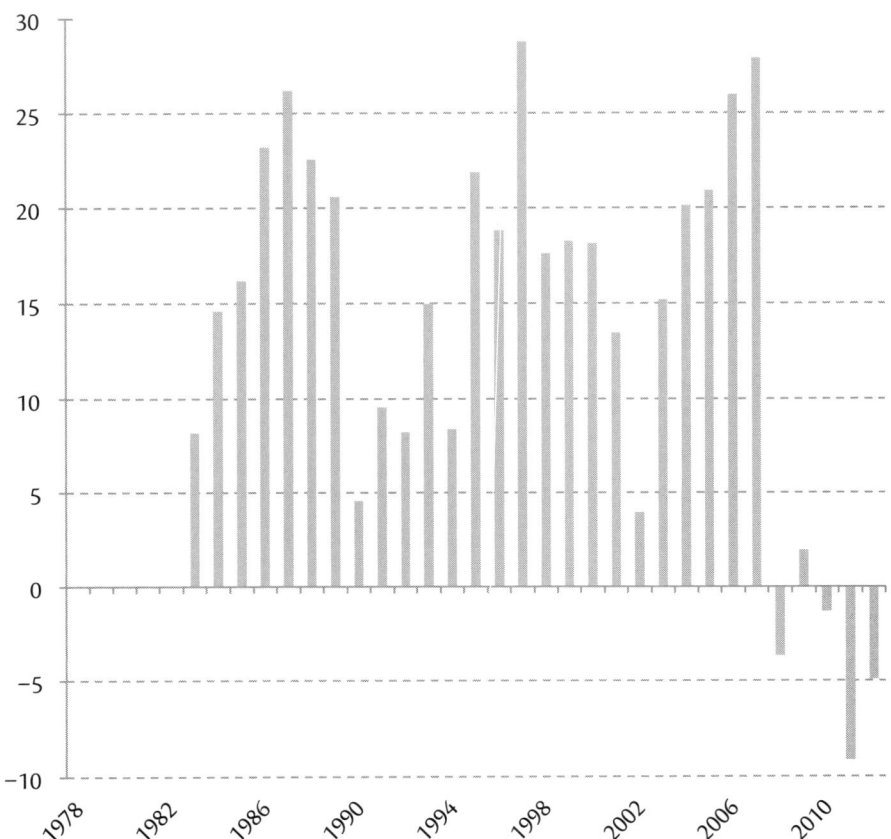

are going to be around long after you and I are gone—so my attitude is 'If you can't beat 'em, might as well join 'em!'

"You need to know one other thing about my buy-and-hold strategy. People who make their living trading stocks are carving off part of their capital base every time they sell. I take great pride in keeping all my unrealized capital gains intact so my capital base also stays intact, which of course allows me to earn more money on my invested capital. I don't understand why anyone would cut the government in on their profits any sooner

Figure 6. Ten-year compound investment returns, 1987–2012 (%)

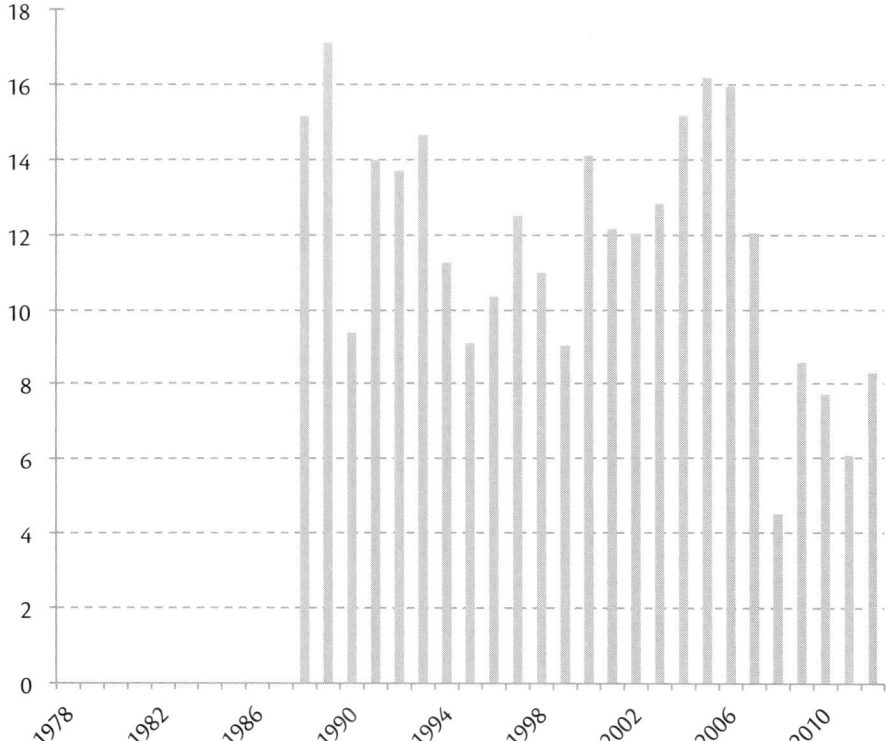

than they had to. Do they not teach compound interest at MBA schools nowadays?"

Good point, Dad, I think as I jot down "RETAIN AS MUCH CAPITAL AS POSSIBLE" on my notepad. His buy-and-hold philosophy has been a cornerstone of his program for more than three decades. It may not be right for everyone, but this low-maintenance approach to portfolio management suits his personality—emphasizing a long-term time horizon, patience and discipline. He has no problem reconciling this investment philosophy with his life philosophy because both operate on the same fundamental principles. No need to get fancy or try to make a quick buck. Just stick with the basics, and let time, compound interest, investment return and tax minimization work their magic.

Dad's sources of investment capital

"Are you ready to talk, son?" I'm eating breakfast. But that's never held Dad back from interrupting me before. He clears his throat and says: "I want to talk about one of my favourite subjects, sources of new investment capital. I love this stuff, kind of like creating money out of thin air."

"Do I have time to finish my breakfast, Dad?"

"Well, I suppose," he says. "But don't dilly-dally, as I might lose my train of thought. I've been doing that more often these days," he says with a laugh. "I wish some guys would get out of bed in the morning so we could put in a decent day. My day is half done before you're ready to start."

We've been bantering like this for as long as I can remember. I'm a little more like my mother, who took life somewhat easier than Dad. If she were still here she would tell him to leave me alone so I could enjoy my breakfast, reminding him that he had absolutely nothing else going on today (or any other day, for that matter). Since she's been gone, breakfasts with Dad aren't quite as leisurely as they used to be, although I sometimes draw them out—just a little—to get a rise out of him.

I haven't quite finished the last spoonful of cereal before Dad jumps in. "Okay, Douglas, let's go back to day one . . ." I look up, pretending to be surprised that he's right there in front of me. "Actually, Dad," I reply, as I push my chair away from the table and stand up, "let's move out to the back porch, where we can sit and chat properly. Come on, let's go." Dad mumbles something, then turns and heads for the door.

We settle into our chairs, and Dad picks up right where he left off. "When I started investing," he continues, "I approached my bank for an $18,000 loan. Doesn't seem like a lot, especially when you consider I was putting in $200,000, but you never know what's going on in a banker's mind. Damn, can you believe it, Bob's last name slips my mind—give me a moment, it'll come." I wait, but it doesn't come. Dad seems mildly annoyed, but he moves on. "Anyway, $18,000 wasn't a big deal for either one of us, but it's the way I wanted to start—nice and slow so I wasn't in too deep in case I had problems. Anyway, I went right to the top—Bob was the manager at my CIBC branch in Claresholm. Bankers never tip their hand, but I think Bob actually liked my idea—although there was no way he was going to show too much enthusiasm. I shudder to think that all of this might not have happened had he not gone to bat for me on that first loan. Make sure you mention his name in the book, you know, give him a little prominence, as the story would be quite different without his initial support.

"The first two sources of capital are your money and the bank's money. Pretty obvious. Some people start leveraging with no 'skin' on the table, but I'm leery of that approach. You've got to make a personal commitment to it, or it's too easy to back out when the first market correction comes along. And we both know they come along more than we'd like to admit," he adds, as we share a nervous chuckle.

"The third potential source of capital is the accumulated tax savings you create from the annual tax deductibility of your interest expense on your leverage loan. Some people like to spend their tax savings, but that defeats the whole purpose of what we're trying to do here. Instead of a yacht or that blowout trip to Vegas, think long term and reinvest these dollars back into your Tax-Free Savings Accounts or RRSP. Remember, the goal here is to create a larger capital base for compound interest to do its thing over the next ten, twenty, thirty and even forty years.

"My fourth source of capital comes from the unrealized gains on my investments," Dad explains. "In the eyes of my banker, these unrealized gains are considered to be capital additions. This reduces my margin ratio, which in turn reduces my level of risk. But better yet, all my money stays intact rather than airmailing it off to Ottawa. Capital retention—that's the whole idea behind my buy-and-hold strategy. Why keep flipping my portfolio over? So I can pay tax every year? No sir, they'll have to wait until I'm good and ready to pay before they see one penny of taxes from me. And don't forget—I'm a very patient, disciplined man," he says, "especially when it comes to paying deferred taxes!"

"I'm not sure if you remember, Douglas, but I owe the government a million dollars—give or take—and this 'interest-free loan' from the government keeps on making me more money every year. I just wish I was little younger . . . I'd try to make another million compliments of the government over the next decade." He stops, smiles and then adds, "Now wouldn't that be the 'icing on the cake'?"

When Dad started his leveraging program in 1978, the cash injection from the bank loan was minimal: only 8% was borrowed money and 92% was his own money. But thirty-five years later, the ratios are dramatically different: 28% is borrowed money (current bank loan); 11% is the government's money (deferred taxes); 59% is accumulated profits (unrealized capital gains); and only a scant 2% is the initial investment (original $200,000).

Figure 7 shows Dad's sources of capital then and now. Here's a breakdown in actual dollars.

Figure 7. Sources of capital, 1978 & 2012

	1978 ($000's)	2012 ($000's)
Original capital	200	200
Bank loan	18	2,650
Accumulated profits	0	5,500
Deffered income taxes	0	1,100
Total investment capital	218	9,300
Net portfolio	200	6,650

Dad's purchasing patterns

By now you know that Dad started his program in 1978 with $200,000 of his own money and an investment loan of $18,000. He really didn't have any additional money to invest after that. Oh, he may have had a few dollars here and there, but for certain nothing after he retired in 1986.

Since Dad didn't have any of his own money to invest, he relied on the growth of his portfolio to create margin room in his program to fund additional investment purchases. From 1978 to 1986, when he retired from the insurance business, Dad borrowed $700,000 to make additional purchases for his portfolio. Although he tended to buy when his portfolio was at its peak value (and he had margin room available), because he made smaller purchases consistently over the nine-year period in a dollar cost averaging manner, he managed to keep his acquisition costs down. The result: an $800,000 retirement "nest egg" by the end of 1986.

Dad wasn't overly active in the buying arena in the first nine years of his retirement. He bought $600,000 of investments from 1987 to 1995 but sold off $550,000, not a strong statement in either direction. I'm not sure if it was because of the drubbing he took on Black Monday in 1987 or because he was just enjoying the freedom of retired life, but for whatever reason, Dad was not in a "buying" mood during this time. No problem: at the end of 1995, eighteen years into his program, his net portfolio had still grown to $2.1 million.

Even though everything was going well, Dad was always looking to refine his strategy. He had a good ally. My brother John was keenly interested in what Dad was up to, so the two of them started to accumulate data on all of the key variables of Dad's program on one rather large spreadsheet. This digital "dashboard" showed Dad everything he needed to know, from how much and when he should be purchasing additional stock to his projected dividend income, interest expense and margin ratio parameters. In short, Dad now had all the tools at his fingertips to manage his strategy in a manner he had never dreamed of.

From 1996 to 2000, Dad purchased just under $1.1 million of new investments. Even though the markets were mixed towards the end of the millennium (with the "Asian" flu of 1998, the tech run-up of 1998 and 1999, and the subsequent tech "bubble" of 2000), Dad still managed to rack up $1.9 million in profits over this five-year period. Evidently his apprenticeship learning the intricacies of John's spreadsheet was time well spent.

Dad was now ready to roll. In 2001, he purchased more than $1 million of investments, and he followed that up with purchases of more than $7.8 million over the next six years, totalling $8.9 million over the seven-year period. He was most active in 2004 and 2005, fortunately backing off a bit in 2006 and 2007. This purchasing pattern may at first glance seem excessive, but it was all done according to plan and tracked fastidiously on the spreadsheet. The results were impressive—profits of $6.7 million for the seven-year period ending 2007.

Then 2008 hit. The year started out okay, but by summer things were softening. All hell broke loose in September. What started as a mortgage crisis in the States quickly turned into a worldwide stock market panic. Dad was obviously more vulnerable than most because of his leveraged position. Unfortunately, the market correction was so fast and severe that Dad didn't have time to react to the downturn. Any thoughts of buying quickly turned to selling. His only option for survival was to sell off rapidly declining assets at whatever prices he could get, and sell he did—to the tune of $8 million over the next six months.

When the market finally bottomed in early March of 2009, Dad went on a buying spree, adding $1.5 million of new investments during the rest of the year, almost a third of the value of his opening gross portfolio. He bought aggressively, reclaiming some of the same names at the "fire sale" prices he'd been forced to sell at just months earlier. Looking back, there's no question this redeployment of capital was the catalyst that saved a program that just months earlier had been on life support.

Perhaps it's more important to look past this period and look at Dad's purchasing patterns over more than thirty years. While it's difficult to look at one aspect of his program in isolation, there's no question that his dollar cost averaging strategy helped him make more consistent, disciplined purchasing decisions and manage the normal emotions of fear and greed that can turn rational investors into irrational investors.

Managing his debt

I've often wondered how Dad stayed comfortable with the growth of his loan, which grew systematically to over $10 million at its peak (see Figure 8). I wanted to hear Dad's story before

I did my own analysis, so I put the question to him on a trip to Lethbridge in the summer of 2012.

"Well, to be honest, Douglas, the loan crept up in value over a long period of time. I started small and didn't pass through a half million of debt until '87, nine years later. Then Black Monday arrived." Dad looks over, goes to talk but stops. Nothing else needs to be said.

"That shook me up pretty badly, so I reduced my debt by roughly $150,000—25% of the $600,000 loan I started the year with. It would take another ten years for me to add an additional $400,000 in debt. I passed through a million of debt in 1997, almost twenty years after walking into CIBC for my initial loan. You can see this whole leveraging thing happened very slowly over a long period of time.

"Anyway," Dad continues, "over the next four years I borrowed another million and a half dollars, taking my debt level to about $2.5 million by the end of 2001. John's spreadsheet made everything systematic, telling me how much I needed to buy to keep my margin ratio within its targeted range, so I felt I was right where I should be.

"Then we had a few good years there where the markets really took off. The spreadsheet told me that I should be buying more stock so I did. In fact, I bought a lot—almost $8 million worth over the next six years, which took my loan to over $10 million in the early part of 2008." He stops for a moment to consider the enormity of the number before going on. "Amazing when you think about it, but it was all done according to plan.

"I'd been matching my money with bank money since 2001," Dad continues. "You may be thinking that I was running my leverage 'engine' a little hard, but remember that I made more than $6 million in those six years . . . so everything was pretty much going by the book—the numbers were big on both sides of the ledger.

"The year 2007 opened my eyes a bit. The market dropped 7% over the year, causing my margin ratio to sneak up to almost 54%. That was higher than I wanted and more than my spreadsheet said it should be. In my defence, the increase was more due to the 7% decline in my portfolio than to me wanting to be above the 50% mark. Remember, when the markets drop in value, my margin ratio goes up, since I'm carrying the same debt load over a smaller portfolio value." He bites his lip. "Managing this ratio in up-market years is easy . . . but it's a real challenge in down-market years, trust me, Douglas.

"Then 2008 came along, nothing but bad news—started in the States but then it spread like a prairie wildfire through the rest of the world. I knew I was in tough but I did the best I could. Unfortunately, that wasn't enough. Damned near lost everything. Can you believe it, Douglas? Thirty years of work *that far*"—he makes a pinching motion with his thumb and index finger—"from going down the drain . . . It seems unfathomable but it almost happened—one wrong move by Paulson down in the States and we could have been back to a '30s-type depression. Oh well," he deadpans, "at least I would have been better prepared for that than most!"

Sensing Dad's discomfort in discussing these dark days, I change the subject slightly. "Who would have ever thought that the markets could get so bad? Heck, even most of the so-called market experts completely misread the depth of the downturn."

Dad nods his head in agreement, then replies, "Well, I certainly didn't see it coming. But what about all those highly paid money managers in Toronto and New York who are backed up by those fancy research departments? Weren't they supposed to have their fingers on the pulse of the investment world? For all their fancy gadgets, they might as well have been sitting downstairs with me looking at BNN." Liking what he just said, Dad turns to me and says, "And you can quote me on that one."

Figure 8. Total debt outstanding, 1978–2012

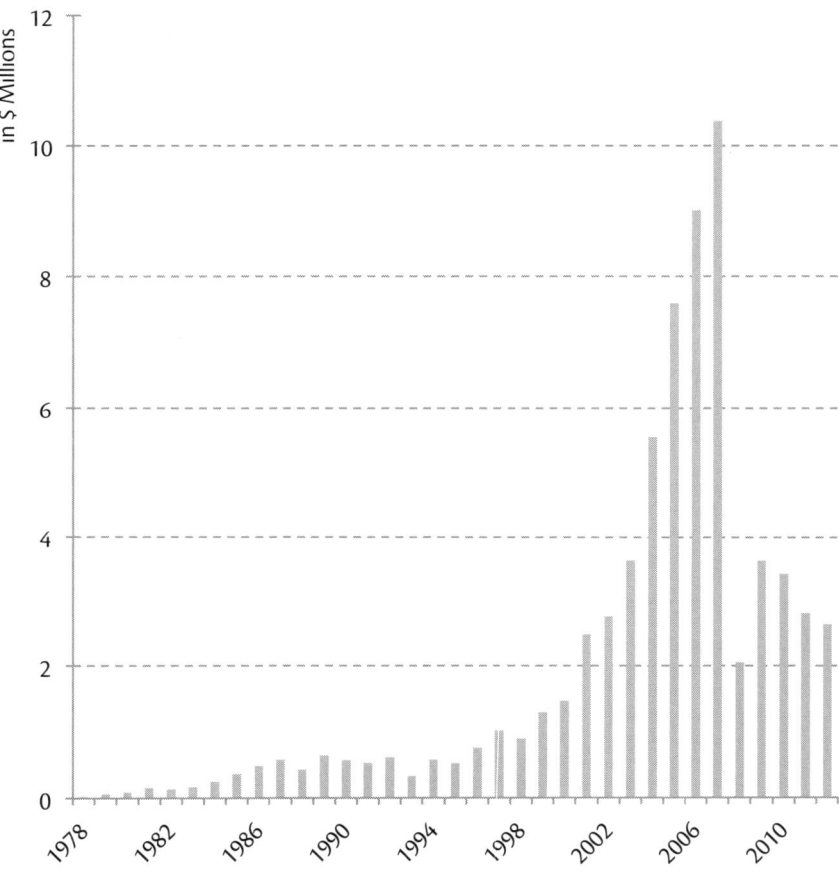

Figure 8 shows Dad's debt outstanding over thirty-five years. Note the extensive use of debt during the period 2001 to 2007. This corresponded with Dad's most profitable years and was followed by his year of worst returns, 2008. Dad's debt level dropped back to its pre-2001 level in 2008, prior to his buying spree in 2009. Since 2010 he's been using his net dividend stream to repay his outstanding loan.

Dad's use of leverage

The following chart (Figure 9) shows Dad's average margin ratios during different periods from 1981 to 2012. I've left out 1978 to 1980 because it took him about three years to get the whole leveraging concept "figured out." Here are my findings:

Figure 9. Average margin ratios, 1981–2012 (%)

1981–2000	32.5
2001–2007	47.6
2008–2009	42.2
2010–2012	32.5

From 1981 to 2000, Dad maintained an average margin ratio of about 33%, or a little over two parts his money and one part bank money. This period included the '81–82 recession, Black Monday in October 1987, his early retirement years of the late '80s and the initial years of working with John's spreadsheet in the late '90s. As I mentioned previously, a margin ratio of 33% turns a 10% unleveraged gain into a 15% leveraged gain, but it also turns a 10% unleveraged loss into a 15% leveraged loss.

By the early 2000s, Dad had been working with John's spreadsheet for almost five years. While he was receiving valuable information on all aspects of his program, one variable in his program was getting more and more of his attention. The problem that Dad encountered in the early years of the new millennium was that his portfolio was growing almost exponentially. Now, this may not sound like much of a problem to you and me, but it created a real dilemma for my dad.

Let me explain. The increasing value of his portfolio meant his relative debt level—and thus his margin ratio—was decreasing. Interest rates had fallen dramatically from those of the '80s and '90s, which reduced Dad's deductible interest expense and margin ratio accordingly. If he did nothing, his dividend income would be greater than his interest expense, resulting in a higher taxable income and a higher tax bill. Ahh . . . more taxes—my dad's Achilles heel.

If Dad wanted to keep his taxes down, he only had one option: increase his debt and his corresponding margin ratio. This of course meant taking more risk and creating the potential for greater return. Always wanting better information before making a decision, Dad thoroughly exhausted John with what-if tax and investment questions. When he finally knew the numbers inside out, he made the decision to increase his margin ratio, thereby increasing both portfolio risk and potential portfolio return.

He decided to move towards a 50% ratio, where half the invested capital would come from the bank and half from him. Over the next seven years, from 2001 to 2007, Dad methodically increased his margin ratio from the previous norm of 33% to about 50% (see Figure 10). This meant that 10% unleveraged returns would turn into 20% leveraged returns and 10% unleveraged losses would turn into 20% losses. This more aggressive margin ratio produced exceptional results between 2001 and 2007: a profit of some $6.7 million and an annual compound rate of return of 22.5%.

September 2008 changed everything. Dad found it increasingly difficult to maintain his margin ratio target of 50%. He was constantly overextended. When his friendly banker called, it wasn't to discuss the weather. With his portfolio listing sideways like a ship taking on water, the only thing Dad could do to keep his margin ratio in balance was to sell stock. He wasn't alone.

We all know what happens to stock prices if everybody is trying to sell at the same time. More sellers, fewer buyers—prices can only go in one direction: down—not exactly the kind of market you want to be selling into. However, Dad was no longer in

Figure 10. Margin ratios, 1978–2012 (%)

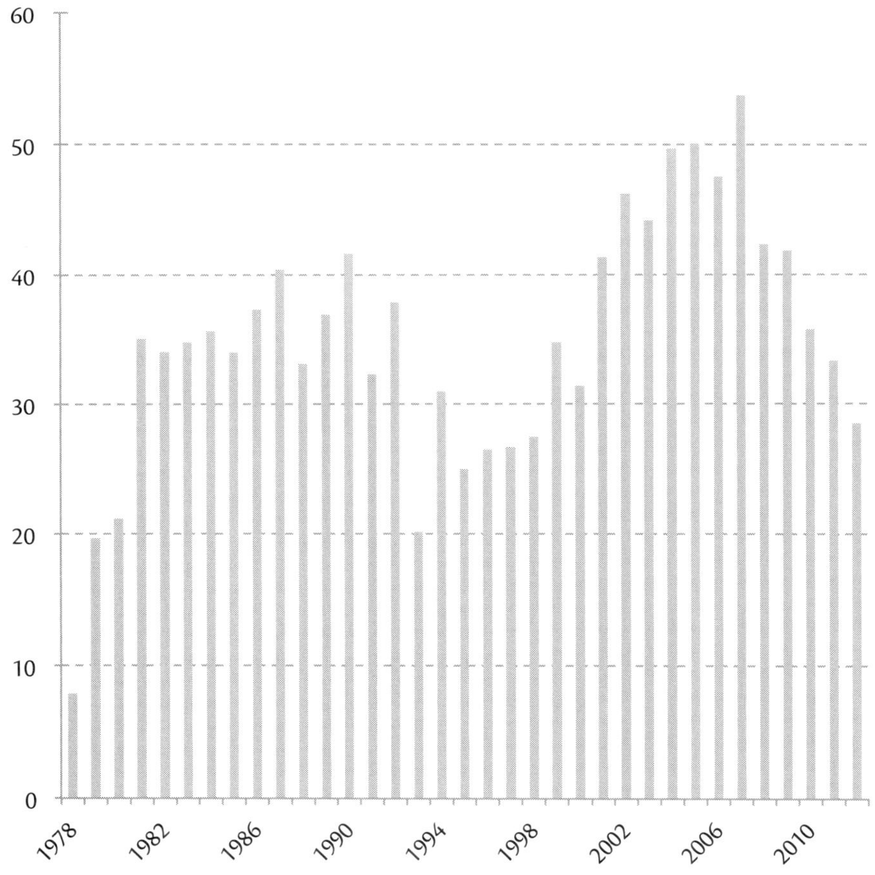

control of his portfolio. Like it or not, his banker was now calling the shots. Dad sold off $8 million of stock over the next six months just to survive. His margin ratio fluctuated wildly during this period, sometimes getting as high as 67%. He ended the year 2008 with a portfolio loss of $5.9 million, but he did manage to get his margin ratio down to a more manageable 42%.

Dad started buying again early in 2009, when stocks were at rock-bottom prices, increasing his debt load by more than $1.5 million—from $2,057,000 at the beginning of the year to $3,638,000 at the end of the year. However, his portfolio growth of $2.35 million more than offset his debt growth and provided an 87% return—his best year ever. His margin ratio remained constant over the year at roughly 43%, even after all the buying he had done.

In early 2010, at age eighty-eight, Dad decided it was time to "put his feet up," as he always liked to say, and properly retire a second time. That meant no more stock purchases. After following a strategy of increasing his debt load to match portfolio growth for more than thirty years, Dad started using his dividend cash flow to pay down his investment loan. He augmented that with a few select stock sales to reduce his debt level to just over $2.8 million by the end of 2011—roughly the same 33% margin level he had averaged over the two decades prior to 2002. By the end of 2012, he had reduced his margin ratio further, to 28%. Figure 10 shows Dad's annual margin ratios from 1978 to 2012. Note the increased ratios starting in 2001 until 2008, and then the decreasing ratios thereafter as Dad started to systematically reduce his debt in 2010.

Cash flow management

Dad has always tried to match his interest expense against his dividend income. When he started investing, this was relatively easy, since the cost of borrowing money was high. Remember, Dad lived through the age of 22% interest rates in the early '80s! A high borrowing cost translates into increased interest expense for tax purposes. This was a negative from a cost perspective, but it may have been a positive from a risk perspective, because it meant

Dad could match his dividend income and interest expense with much less debt. As interest rates declined over the years, Dad had to increase his debt load to maintain this cash flow relationship.

He followed this strategy diligently until 2008, when margin ratio management took precedence over everything else Dad was doing. By the end of 2009, Dad's cash flow had increased significantly, even though he had gone on a buying spree during the year. Three things caused this to happen.

First, the Bank of Canada moved aggressively to stabilize the economy with even lower interest rates. This reduced the cost of his loans to unheard-of levels. Savers bore the brunt of this move, but it was "manna from heaven" for borrowers like Dad, who was now paying less than 3% on his investment loan.

Second, dividend payouts remained basically the same. Despite the severe economic challenges faced by corporations, many, including Canadian banks, chose to continue their previous payout policy to maintain investor confidence in their stock. Dad's dividend payout from his portfolio increased to about 4%, which was significantly higher than his borrowing cost.

Third, Dad stopped making further stock purchases by the end of 2009, so his debt level was reduced relative to the increasing value of his recovering portfolio. The result? His margin ratio declined.

The cumulative effect of these three factors on Dad's cash flow was significant. The days of matching dividend income and interest expense were now in the rear-view mirror. Instead, he now had more than $250,000 of net cash flow per year available to service his outstanding debt—and that's exactly what he did. By the end of 2011, his margin ratio had fallen to 33%—just in time to celebrate his ninetieth birthday. It's currently about 27% and declining every month, as Dad never misses making a $20,000 payment.

There it is—Dad's investment story by the numbers. Now that you have a solid understanding of his investment program, let's take a look at Dad's tax philosophy and the various strategies he employs to keep his investment gains safely tucked into his own pocket, away from the outstretched hands of you-know-who.

Chapter 13

It's Not What You Earn, It's What You Keep

D AD'S A SEASONED PRO AT THE TAX GAME. He's at the top of his form and has been there for a long time—perennial all-star on the all-time, all-Canadian tax team. This is a team that you should strive to make. You won't be on the CRA's Christmas card list, but don't worry about that; you probably don't send them a card either.

Dad focuses on three key strategies to keep his tax bill down:

1. Reducing current taxes
2. Deferring tax to the future
3. Minimizing tax on retirement income

Reducing current taxes

Dad has made tax minimization a priority for as long as I can remember. His focus on matching his tax-deductible interest expense against dividend income has saved him well over a million dollars in taxes over the last thirty-five years. In the past few years he has deliberately reduced his debt and corresponding deductible interest expense, so this matching strategy is a thing of the past. However, because the majority of his income is dividends, he still has a low average tax rate of 16%—not a bad rate for a retiree with over $300,000 of annual income.

Dad is the only person I know who still has copies of his tax returns dating back to 1948. That's sixty-five years, so you know he takes this game seriously. I've put together a table (Figure 11) showing his net cash flow and income taxes paid for the period 2007 to 2012. Follow along with me, and I'll show you some very pertinent information.

Take a look at the 2007 tax year. Dad's investment loan peaked at over $10 million. He had $570,000 of tax-deductible interest expense and $6,000 of OAS clawback against income of $556,000, resulting in negative cash flow of $20,000.

You could argue that he lost some tax efficiency in 2007 since his interest expense didn't result in tax savings on the last $20,000 of income, but that's probably splitting hairs. Regular tax calculations resulted in zero taxes payable, but when the tax department calculated on the basis of Alternative Minimum Tax, he ended up owing about $6,000 in taxes for the year.

The year 2008 was extraordinary. To survive the market downturn, Dad sold a significant portion of his portfolio. This sell-off triggered a taxable capital gain of $203,000 and a tax bill of some $82,000. Tough medicine for a guy who had just lost $6 million! However, to lose all that money and still have taxable

Figure 11. Net cash flow & income taxes paid, 2007–2012 (in $)

	2007	2008	2009	2010	2011	2012
Cash in						
Pension	45,713	43,688	37,904	38,961	39,229	39,756
Actual dividends	461,653	505,130	315,299	339,501	336,740	349,266
Capital gains	23,415	203,063	0	0	0	0
Other	25,046	24,796	5,484	3,765	2,159	1,011
Total cash in	555,827	776,677	358,687	382,227	378,128	390,033
Cash out						
Interest expense	569,732	416,393	57,546	72,805	81,517	68,642
OAS clawback	5,952	6,082	6,203	6,222	6,368	6,511
Total cash out	575,684	422,475	63,749	79,027	87,585	75,153
Cash flow before taxes	−19,857	354,202	294,938	303,200	290,543	314,880
Income taxes paid	5,952	82,001	44,277	45,266	43,294	50,465
Net cash flow	25,814	272,201	250,661	257,934	247,244	264,415
Income taxes / cash flow before taxes (%)	−30.0	23.2	15.0	14.9	14.9	16.0

capital gains gives you some idea of how much tax deferral he had built up over the years.

The year 2009 was a year of transition. Although Dad purchased a significant amount of stock early in the year, his deductible interest expense of $58,000 was now just over 18% of his $315,000 dividend income.

The years 2009 through 2011 reflect this increased net cash flow as he averaged $44,000 of taxes (15% tax rate) on average taxable cash flow of $296,000 over this three-year period, resulting in after-tax cash flow of $252,000. In 2012, Dad paid $50,000 in taxes, or 16% tax, on cash flow before taxes of $315,000.

You can see that the combination of a growing dividend stream and a diminishing interest expense (due to his ongoing debt repayment) is increasing his net cash flow and income taxes payable. However, 16% tax on more than $300,000 of taxable cash flow is still extremely tax efficient and a credit to a lifetime of astute tax planning.

Deferring tax to the future

Remember Dad's 98-cent dollars—the kind he likes so much? You achieve these when you "buy and hold" stocks for long periods of time and defer tax far into the future, eventually paying tax with inflation-reduced dollars. Dad loaded up on bank stocks in the 1990s and has held them ever since.

In early 2009, I had to break the news to him that John and I had done the math and it looked like it would be necessary to sell at least some of these beloved stocks to save his overall program. I remember his reaction well: "Son, sell them if you have to, but that just breaks my heart. I feel like I'm just giving away good solid companies for pennies on the dollar. I don't understand what's going on—these markets make absolutely no sense to me."

At that time, the big concern was whether banks would continue to pay dividends to their investors. Historically, Canadian banks have never missed a dividend payment, so we felt they would do everything they could to maintain this record. But we were also worried that nothing was sacred (in the hockey world even Gretzky got traded!) and companies would do whatever was necessary to stay afloat. Fortunately, the banks kept their dividend policies intact, continuing to pay their full quarterly dividend payouts. Furthermore, Dad didn't have to sell as many bank shares as we had first thought. Today these stocks represent 70% of his portfolio and pay out approximately 4% in annual dividends.

Let's take a look at how his "Big Three" bank holdings (Bank of Montreal, Bank of Nova Scotia and CIBC) have performed over the years (see Figure 12).

Figure 12. Big Three bank holdings: Capital gains analysis

	Cost ($000's)	Current Value ($000's)	Gain ($000's)	Gain (%)
BMO	157	903	746	475
BNS	892	2,952	2,060	231
CIBC	446	2,318	1,872	420
Total	1,495	6,173	4,678	313

His original investment in these long-term holdings has grown from $1,495,000 to $6,173,000, resulting in unrealized gains of $4,678,000, a 313% increase on their original value. His two oldest holdings, BMO and CIBC, have more than quintupled, while the baby of the group, BNS, has more than tripled in value, up 231%.

What Dad really likes about these gains is that he doesn't have to pay any capital gains tax until he disposes of them. This is the equivalent of an interest-free loan from the government for the amount of tax that he'll eventually have to pay. Alberta's tax rate on capital gains is 20%, so Dad owes income tax of $944,000 on these gains. But in the meantime, Dad gets to use these deferred taxes owing to make more money. Even better, Dad is in control of when he wants to trigger this future tax obligation. No sale of stock, no taxable event. What's not to like about that?

How much is this tax deferral actually worth? Well, let's look at the numbers. He has earned 11.8% annually over the past twenty-five years, but for easy figuring let's assume he's made 10% annually over this period. He currently earns about 4% annual dividends on these stocks, so let's also assume he's made another 6% annual capital growth on his portfolio. On average, based on his current deferral, this works out to just under $40,000 of additional taxable dividends and about $60,000 of additional tax-deferred capital growth on this deferral each and every year. That's around $100,000 a year in Dad's pocket, less $6,000 tax (15% tax on the taxable $40,000) simply because he refuses to sell his winning stocks. Not a bad return on money that technically isn't even his.

Minimizing tax on retirement income

From 2010 on, Dad started to use any dividend income remaining after paying interest expenses to reduce his outstanding loan. For the years 2010 and 2011, his dividend income averaged about $338,000 per year, while his interest expense averaged a little over $77,000 a year. This left a net cash flow of $261,000 per year available for loan repayment. His average taxable income for these years was $297,000, and he averaged approximately $44,000 of income tax per year—about 14.9% of actual income earned. His average tax rate increased to 16% in 2012 and should remain within one or two percentage points of this for the rest of his life. Assuming Dad holds his investments until he dies (about a 99.9% probability!), there will be a deemed disposition of his investments on his death and the government will collect their million dollars of tax owing on his accrued capital gains.

For the sake of comparison, let's assume that Dad didn't pursue his leveraged investment strategy but instead accumulated the same assets within an RRSP or defined contribution pension plan to provide for the same retirement income that he currently receives from his program.

I ran a tax projection on Dad earning $297,000 from RRIF or pension income and found that he would pay annual income taxes of $110,000, or 37% of his income. Compare this to Dad's $44,000 tax bill and 15% average tax rate. The math is pretty simple. Dad's long-term tax planning is saving him about $66,000 each and every year in taxes. This increases his net after-tax cash flow from $187,000 per year to $253,000 per year. Let me tell you—$66,000 additional annual income is a lot of money for any retiree.

This shows you how important it is to start your retirement tax and income planning during your accumulation years and not when you're actually retired. Your tax saving potential may be more or less than this, but whatever it is, you're always better off with the money in your pocket rather than in the hands of the government.

Remember, once it's gone, it's gone forever.

Chapter 14

Was It All Worthwhile?

NOW THAT WE'VE DISSECTED ALL ASPECTS OF DAD'S INVESTMENT PROGRAM, WE NEED TO ANSWER THE BIG QUESTION: WAS IT ALL WORTHWHILE? Were the rewards enough to offset the risks he took? We know one thing for sure: there's no free lunch with leveraged investing. Since Dad took more than normal risk, he needed higher than normal market returns to justify taking this additional risk.

In the end, it all comes down to the numbers, so here they are (see Figure 13).

From 1987 to 2011, during his twenty-five-year retirement, Dad made an additional 4.4% return from his leverage strategy, increasing his unleveraged return from 7.4% to 11.8%. How significant is this? Well, if you check back to the compound interest section (pages 54 to 59), you'll see that money quadruples over forty years assuming an additional annual 4% return. When you add in Dad's pre-retirement years of 1978 to 1986 as well as 2012, the returns attributed to leverage over thirty-five years are slightly better than the 4.4% additional return earned in his retirement years. This puts him well on the way to quadrupling the returns he would have made over forty years had he *not* followed his leveraging strategy.

Figure 13. Margin ratios & five-year compound returns, 1987–2011

	Average Margin Ratio (%)	Average Compound Five-Year Return (%)	Compound Five-Year Return on Dad's Dollars (%)	Compound Five-Year Return on Borrowed Dollars (%)
1987 – 1991	36.8	9.6	6.1	3.5
1992 – 1996	28.1	18.8	13.5	5.3
1997 – 2001	32.3	13.5	9.1	4.4
2002 – 2006	47.6	26	13.6	12.4
2007 – 2011	41.4	−9.1	−5.3	−3.8
Averages	37.2	11.8	7.4	4.4
Percentage of total return		100	62.8	37.2

Numbers like this are rarely seen in any field. We've all seen excellent results achieved over shorter time frames, but how often have you seen outstanding results achieved in any endeavour over a thirty-five-year period? It's difficult for a son to fairly assess the success of a father's achievement, so I won't even try.

All I know is that Dad has created more than $9 million of wealth since 1978—most of it in his retirement years. Not bad for a guy who was just looking for something stimulating to do in his golden years. I'm sure other dads have done greater and lesser things throughout their lives, but I happen to be pretty proud of this particular dad.

Chapter 15

Lessons Learned From My Dad

I T'S GETTING LATE, AND I HAVEN'T PACKED YET. My shirts
are draped across the bed and my suitcase sits open, ready to
be filled. But instead of packing, I've been hunched over the
desk in Dad's guest room, scratching out words and scribbling
corrections, in a mad rush to finish my edits before time runs
out. I'm leaving tomorrow, early morning. Drive to Calgary, fly
to Vancouver. Long day ahead. I assured Dad I wasn't going to
work late tonight. We were at it all day, reviewing all aspects of
my work, trying to ensure I had everything I needed before I left.
We're at the point where I have to start pulling everything together. And that's turning out to be a daunting prospect.

I have more charts and graphs than I'll ever need, more bullet points than I'll ever have space in the book to cover. My problem isn't a lack of information; it's information overload. There are more than three decades of investment history here, in what has become a bulging folder of detailed jottings and notes to self. How do I process this mass of information, condense it down to what's really important, and then present it in a manner that people can really understand—and perhaps more importantly, put to practical use? Right now the process feels overwhelming.

Dad and I worked straight through dinner. I didn't even notice the time until Dad reported that his stomach was growling. No wonder, I thought, when I glanced at the kitchen clock; it was almost 7:30 p.m. "Dad," I said, "we've got to eat something. It's getting late." Ready with a joke as always, Dad replied: "Well, there is that little pizza place, what's the name? They deliver, I think?" He smirked, remembering the pizza box he had thrown out in the morning. Pizza two nights in a row? That would be a personal record. But hey, if it meant we could keep working . . .

At 9:00 p.m. sharp, Dad started to get up from the table. "Douglas," he said, "I'm heading to bed. It's an early morning for both of us, and I've completely run out of gas." He rounded the table and put his hand on my shoulder. I felt his gentle squeeze and the way he sort of leans on you when he does it, to steady himself. I felt his touch, the connection, but I was still focused on the last chart we had been working on.

"Good night, son," Dad said, recognizing that I was lost in my notes. I mumbled something back. Then I remembered it was my last night here, my last night with Dad for a while, and I snapped out of my thoughts. I looked up and locked eyes with him, then watched a little smile spread across his face as he saw me acknowledge that I'd heard him. I smiled back. He looks content, I thought—happy, actually. This book thing has been a great project for him.

"Good night, Dad," I replied. "I'll see you in the morning, bright and early." He grunted and then started down the hall. I scooped up my notes and shuffled them into a loose pile. I stood up, tucked the pages under my arm, did a quick check to make sure the patio door was locked, and clicked off the kitchen light as I passed by. "Just a half-hour more," I assured myself, as I headed for the guest room.

That was nearly three hours ago. I've been writing non-stop ever since. Now I'm tired. I massage my neck with my left hand, bobbing my head from side to side, as if that will relieve the tension. My body is telling me it's time to stop, to sleep.

I sit back in the chair and sigh. The night air coming through the partially open window is cold but I find it invigorating. I've had good weather here all week, sunny and warm during the day and right around freezing at night. That's all supposed to change as an early-season snowstorm brewing on the west coast is forecast to hit this area sometime in the morning.

I walk over to the window. Outside, the neighbourhood is quiet. People who live here probably don't even notice the quietness, but I do. It's one of the things I'm most aware of when I come here: the stillness of the place, especially compared to downtown Vancouver, where I live.

Dad claims that one of the biggest issues he has coming to my place in Vancouver is the level of noise in the city. According to him, the city's just too darn loud. "How's a fellow supposed to think," he once asked me, "when there's a constant clanging and banging of traffic, right outside your door? They might as well be right here in your living room." I just chuckled and told him that after a while you get used to it. "Well, I sure couldn't," he retorted. To which I replied: "Dad, you lived in a granary, for Pete's sake! A plywood shack with no plumbing, during the depths of a Saskatchewan winter! If you could handle that, then I'm sure you could handle the noise from a few cars passing by." But he just shook his head.

The other thing I notice when I come out to visit Dad is the night sky. You still get a real prairie sky here—that deep, expansive black canvas that sparkles with thousands of stars. Being able to see the stars has always been important to Dad. He once told me that when he was young he would sometimes sneak out at night with a blanket, so he could lie on his back in the field next to the house and gaze at the night sky.

"You know, Douglas," he said, "as a boy, seeing the stars at night was completely normal for me. Growing up, I just took it for granted. Then I moved to Saskatoon and suddenly I couldn't see them anymore. And that's when I realized that it takes darkness—real darkness—to allow you to see the stars. In the city, people just keep adding more lights, which of course block out the stars. Pretty soon, people forget that the stars even exist, even though they're right above our heads.

"Sometimes," he went on, "people can't see what's obvious, what's right in front of them, because they've got too much stuff going on. Too many distractions. Too many lights, too much sound, too much of everything all buzzing around at the same time. Well, you know what my cure for that is? Just turn it off—all of it, everything—and head outside. Then look up. Let the darkness allow you to see the stars. That way you know you're seeing what's really out there."

I thought about that for a while. A real Prairie philosophy. "That's some real fatherly wisdom, Dad," I replied. "It's going in the book for sure." I said it with sincerity, but the look on Dad's face made it clear he thought I was joking. "No, really, Dad, it's a good observation. Maybe it could be a theme? You know, about stripping away everything else so you can focus on what's really essential."

Dad grunted. "Maybe, Douglas," he replied, "but that's your job, figuring out what goes where, the themes and such. I'll leave that to you. That's why you're getting paid the big bucks," he added with a little smirk. "I know it's a big job, but I'm totally comfortable with your ability to pull it all together."

With those words still ringing in my head, I drop the curtain and turn around. The pile of papers on the desk taunts me. I'm frustrated at having to stop, to leave things undone, but I'm too tired to do anything more tonight. I look over at the bed and see the shirts, still lying there. Okay, I sigh. Time to get packing. I start loosely folding my shirts and laying them inside the suitcase, tucking in stray sleeves quickly, without attention to detail. I stuff my socks in the side pouch, flip over the flap and zip it up. Worst packing job ever, but I'm too tired to care. I throw back the covers, slide in between the sheets and shut off the bedside lamp. The room falls into darkness.

I close my eyes, but I can't seem to calm my thoughts. My mind is still throwing around ideas. What goes where? How does it all connect? It's like I'm staring at a jumble of puzzle pieces, with no idea how to fit them together. I can't seem to stop thinking, so I open my eyes and stare into the darkness. I'm not going to be able to sleep until I sort this out. But how?

As my eyes adjust, I notice that the room really isn't as dark as it had first appeared. I can see the outlines of the desk and the chair, even though the lights are off. I roll over to face the window. The curtain is still slightly open, and I can see moonlight filtering in from outside. I realize that I need to fix that curtain, or it'll distract me and I'll never get to sleep. Then suddenly it clicks. I know what I have to do.

I throw back the covers and jump out of bed. I race towards the bedroom door, snatching my bathrobe off the hook. I pull it over one shoulder, then the other, my slippered feet leading me down the hall and around the corner, through the family room. I reach the patio door, flip the latch and step outside. The cold air hits me, causing my body to straighten, but I keep moving. The motion light clicks on, and light floods the backyard. I keep walking as far away from the house as I can. After a few more strides I stop, wrapping my bathrobe a little tighter to ward off the chill in the air. Then, wait for it . . . click. The light cuts out. I stand still for a moment, savouring the darkness as my eyes slowly adjust. Then I look up.

The stars are right there; it feels like I could reach up and touch them. There must be thousands of them! I tip my head back even farther to take in more of the night sky. Dad's right. You do need real darkness to be able to see the stars. I stare for a few minutes, dazzled by the night sky. It's true: sometimes you just need to stop what you're doing—cut out all the clutter—and look up at the stars. It helps you focus on what's really out there, what's really important.

How do I summarize more than three decades of investment history in a final chapter and do justice to the story? What am I really trying to achieve? What is my reader looking for? Then it hits me: give them practical ideas to move forward. Give them the tools so they too can feel confident enough to begin their own investment journey, creating wealth and a more secure future as they go. Don't get too fancy, and make sure they're getting good value for their money. That's been important to my dad ever since we started talking about this project.

I realize that I don't need to say everything. All I need to do is show people the guiding principles of Dad's story. I've given them all the analysis they'll ever need to understand what leveraged investing and sound tax planning can and cannot do for them. I hear Dad's voice in my mind: *Just strip it all back, son, and let them see the stars.*

I stay outside a bit longer, hoping for a shooting star, a meteor shower or something equally cosmic—something to signal that I've figured it out and everything will fit together as it should. Then I hear Dad's voice in the back of my mind: *Don't push your luck, son. You've picked up more insight in one stargazing session than many others pick up in a lifetime.*

Okay, Dad. You're right. I turn to go back inside. The motion light clicks on again, illuminating the backyard with light, reminding me that it's midnight and I'm standing outside in the freezing cold. As I step back into the house, I feel a sense of confidence welling up inside me. I know now what I need to do: share Dad's wisdom through a number of simple truths he's taught me over the years.

My list isn't exhaustive by any means, nor is it meant to be. But if I can somehow give you just one "gem," something that resonates enough for you to say, "Hey, I've been talking about getting my financial affairs in order for a long time. It's now time for action," then I'm satisfied. And you know what? Dad will be too.

1. First things first—save your money

Remember that ING commercial on TV where the banker with the great voice orders you to "save your money"? Well, other than the Dutch accent, my dad could have filled in for the guy and not missed a beat. Reading this book, you might get the sense that my dad is a risk-taker, throwing his money around in the rough-and-tumble world of stock market investing. But nothing could be further from the truth.

Sure, investing in the market is inherently risky. But Dad has always had a plan—and he has spent the past thirty-five years perfecting it. As a result, his portfolio has grown beyond his wildest expectations—from $200,000 in 1978 to around $7 million today. Add the $2 million he's given away to his family, and over that time he has created wealth of about forty-five times his initial investment.

In spite of all this, the first thing Dad would advise any investor to do would be to pay down their non-deductible debt and start a regular savings program. Better yet, start a monthly investment program so that your good saving habit becomes a good investing habit. Other than giving money away to his children and paying his annual tax bill, Dad has never taken money out for his personal gratification. Any gains that have been earned have been reinvested back into his portfolio.

2. Remember, not all debt is equal

If ever there was a poster boy for living frugally and minimizing consumer debt, it would be my father. Dad has preached this lifestyle for as long as I can remember, which is why I was a little surprised when he announced in 1978 that he was going to be borrowing money to invest in the stock market.

At first I wasn't sure this was a good idea. But Dad was. He understood the unique flexibility of debt and the difference between good and bad debt. Some debt buys short-term satisfaction, while other debt helps build long-term security and peace of mind. Likewise, some debt is tax deductible, some is not. How we manage both types of debt can dramatically impact our long-term financial security. Too much credit card debt, for example, can result in a lifetime of playing catch-up.

Good debt, on the other hand, is used to purchase long-term assets—things like a family home to live in or investments that compound to create wealth. As with many things in life, when it comes to debt, moderation is the key. Too much good debt can quickly turn bad if it's not used wisely. A monster house with like-sized payments? Not good. A leveraged investment program that goes beyond your ability to comfortably service the debt, even though the debt is tax deductible? Definitely a no-no. Remember, wise, planned debt decisions can enhance your life while unwise debt decisions can make your life a living hell. Choose well.

3. Know your investor personality

Successful traders often report that they love the rush that comes with short-term trading. Those who *aren't* successful don't find the rush quite as exhilarating. In fact, au contraire, they don't get any rush at all. It didn't take Dad long to realize that short-term trading wasn't for him. He isn't a guy who revels in making high-pressure, split-second decisions to "buy this" or "sell that," often with insufficient or inaccurate information. And he sure isn't someone who wants to be second-guessing every decision, asking himself "what if?" dozens of times a day.

Individual stock prices are affected by a wide range of variables, from dot-com booms and busts to Y2K scares to world economic events, credit issues and government deficit woes. Dad always felt that trying to connect these dots was best left to the "big boys," as he calls them—those young, gung-ho market analyst types in New York and Toronto who are really plugged in to the investment scene.

"I would never be able to compete with those guys," he told me during one of our afternoon chats. "Just look at all the latest doodads and gadgets those young bucks have nowadays, tied to their data streams and who knows what else they receive on a 'real time' basis, whatever the hell that actually means." He grunted and abruptly slapped the table. "No sir, there's no point in me trying to be someone I'm not. The best thing I can do is to quietly go about my business of investing for the long term and leave the short-term trading to the big boys."

I can't stress this point enough. You need to know your own investor personality and ensure that your financial, tax and investment planning reflects who you are and how much risk you're comfortable with. There's no point spending the time and effort developing an investment strategy that doesn't match your personality. It won't hold up.

If you prefer a slow and steady path, then setting up a high-risk investment program is a fast lane to a nervous breakdown. First and foremost, be true to yourself. Having to endure sleepless nights worrying about whether you will still be solvent at sunrise isn't my idea of a good investment strategy—and it certainly isn't my idea of a fulfilling retirement. So keep it simple and be realistic about what you want and what you are willing to do to achieve your goals.

4. Understand leveraged investing inside and out

Leveraging is not without risk. The goal of leveraging is to amplify your investment gains. But leveraging not only amplifies gains—it also amplifies losses. So if regular stock market fluctuations cause you to lose sleep at night, don't even think about leveraged investing.

Stock markets, by their very nature, are volatile. And some days it's difficult to imagine that world markets will ever go up. But as Dad reminds me, that's what people were saying during the Great Depression . . . and we've had a lot of economic growth and market upswings since then. Furthermore, Dad's recovery after the global economic meltdown of 2008–09 is testament to the fact that, although there are pauses, and even sigificant setbacks in economic growth, the world eventually regains momentum and moves forward. People still get up and go to work, with the goal of making their lives better.

So if you're willing to educate yourself on the risks and rewards of leveraged investing, then you're ready to make an educated decision about whether it should be included in your retirement plans. But remember, leveraged investing is definitely not for everyone.

5. Start early, start late, but start

One of Dad's biggest regrets was not starting his leveraged investment program earlier in life. And now, after having read his story, I hope you can see why. No need to worry about how much you start with. The most important thing is to start.

Conversely, don't panic if you're slow out of the gate. After all, you could argue that at the age of fifty-seven, my dad was a "late bloomer." But thirty-five years on, he seems to be doing fine. Time can heal many ailments. So remember: big, small, early, late—it doesn't matter. Nothing happens until you actually start.

6. Focus on a few key principles

Dad's approach to wealth accumulation has pretty much mirrored his approach to life. He has always placed a strong emphasis on a few core investment and tax concepts, rather than getting caught up or carried away with anything too flashy or trendy. He's the same disciplined, patient investor, no matter what the market conditions. This may be his greatest attribute and the biggest reason for his incredible success.

Dad developed his program based on his knowledge of compound interest and the role capital retention plays in long-term wealth creation. The more capital you retain, the more compound interest works on your behalf. Dad integrated investment and tax planning strategies into his program exceptionally well to systematically create long-term, tax-efficient capital growth.

Has he been successful? The numbers tell the story, so here they are one more time: a compound annual return of 11.8% over his twenty-five-year retirement, with 4.4% directly attributed to the leveraging part of his program. You be the judge.

7. When it comes to investing, think decades, not years

Dad has always been a buy-and-hold guy. This strategy fits his personality. He grew up immersed in the seasonal cycles of sowing and reaping that mark life on the farm. He saw that the only way to prosper was to have a long-term perspective, develop a realistic game plan, and then work the plan until you get your desired results.

One of the similarities I see between farming and investing is that sometimes you can do everything right and still not get your desired outcome. In farming there are no shortcuts. It doesn't matter how carefully you planted the seeds if the rain doesn't fall. In times like these, a farmer just has to be patient and wait. The best strategy in years like this is to simply keep dealing with the things that *can* be controlled—and let Mother Nature take care of everything else. Sometimes she cooperates, and sometimes she doesn't.

When it came to investing, it was only natural that Dad would bring a farming perspective to his portfolio. He doesn't spend a lot of time trying to predict short-term market movement. From day one, his philosophy centred on buying reputable companies that had a track record of stable long-term growth along with a growing dividend stream. You may want to adopt the same philosophy.

8. To maximize portfolio growth, minimize your tax bill

With regard to taxes, Dad knows what's important. When he talks, I listen—and so should you. Not only does he understand how important tax reduction is, he has also put this knowledge to good use, creating millions of dollars in tax savings and deferral.

His tax planning focuses on three strategies:

1. Minimizing current taxation
2. Deferring tax to the future
3. Reducing taxation on retirement income

Remember, tax planning is a marathon, not a sprint. Dad's experience demonstrates that consistent tax planning creates tremendous tax savings. His current annual retirement income is about $300,000 and he pays roughly $50,000 in taxes, an average tax rate of about 16%. Regular pension or RRIF income in the same amount would cost $110,000, so his tax planning is now saving him roughly $60,000 a year in taxes. Tax savings like this are truly remarkable, but remember, it takes time to achieve this type of tax efficiency. The sooner you start planning to reduce your taxes, the sooner you'll see a lower tax bill.

9. Have patience—it's not just for farmers

My dad has a good temperament for investing. He is disciplined, patient and thinks long term—character traits that were instilled in him growing up in that small Prairie farming community. Anyone who knows anything about farming knows that while there may be a lot of ways to make a quick buck in the world, farming isn't one of them.

Farming is a multi-stage process where everything has to go right every step of the way. You have to plant the right seeds at the right time in the right location. You have to watch over the tiny green shoots with care, all the while being on guard for things that could potentially harm the plants you've so carefully nurtured. You have to harvest at just the right time—not too early and not too late. There's no room for short-term thinking in the agricultural arena. Like it or not, farmers are in it for the long haul.

An outlook like this—one that emphasizes patient, long-term thinking—is probably the best attitude a farmer can have. I'm also convinced it's one of the best attributes an investor can have. It has certainly worked for Dad. As previously mentioned, over the past thirty-five years, he's created more than $9 million out of that initial $200,000. Any farmer would be overjoyed with a return of that magnitude.

Just in case you still believe it takes a financial whiz to succeed in the market, let me share a brief story with you that I think illustrates why just staying in the game is what ultimately matters.

My mother was never a numbers person. As a result, she didn't care one bit about Dad's investment program. She loved the outdoors and she loved music—she was a self-taught pianist whose natural rhythm made old-time swing tunes "jump" off the piano. Anyway, I don't know how or when, but somewhere along the line Dad convinced Mom that it would be good to have some money in her name. Dad's reasoning was that having her own investments would help keep their family tax rate down as well as give her a little "something" in case anything ever happened to him. In his mind, it was simple: he'd lend her the seed capital to start and help her arrange for any additional financing required as her portfolio grew. All she had to do was sit on it for the long term.

Mom wasn't sure. But after much cajoling from Dad—and probably more than a little negotiation on her part—Mom agreed to go ahead with his plan, as long as she didn't have to do anything or be overly involved with paperwork, which she didn't like. Excellent decision, Mom! When she died in 2006, she had a grand total of $574 in the bank. But the investment account Dad had set up for her had grown to $1,636,021. She hadn't put a dime in!

This "invest and forget it" example serves to highlight the fundamental point that what really matters is not financial wizardry, but time and basic mathematics. And you don't have to be a numbers person to see the benefits of that.

10. Hang in there when times get tough

Successful investing isn't easy. You have to have a plan. And you have to stick to the plan—not just in the "everything's going great" times, but also in the "world may be ending" times that are bound to come along. Remember, just as in farming, investors can do all the right things and still not get the right results. Dad has seen more than one or two crops that have been slow to germinate turn into bountiful harvests. The important thing to remember about farming and investing is not to become discouraged in the short run or give up.

When I look back over my dad's thirty-five years in the investment world, I'm reminded how steady he has been through the thick and the thin. When I ask him about this, he just shrugs and says: "Douglas, if you're going to be in this business, you better have a pretty good game plan and a strong belief in what you're doing, because you're going to be constantly challenged along the way."

As he says this, I'm reminded of the hundreds of phone calls we've had over the years talking about his personal trials and tribulations. I marvel at how focused, disciplined and patient he's been through good and bad markets and good and bad times. I think of his persistence and resilience in tough, tough markets.

And then it strikes me. At age seventeen, Dad survived a harsh Prairie winter in a granary, with only a small wood stove and a plywood bunk. I can't think of anything more rudimentary than that. He watched his parents survive the 1930s dustbowl and come out the other side. The machinery and land loans eventually got paid off. He learned that tough times don't last, but that tough people do. So when it came to leveraged stock investing, he was well prepared. In fact, you could argue he'd been preparing for it his whole life.

Has he been through tough times in the markets? Sure. Was he ever discouraged? You bet. But he had developed a powerful tool to help him through it: the right attitude. Through it all, he's always gritted his teeth and carried on, just like his parents did. And you know what? The stock markets eventually got better, just as life on the farm eventually got better. And that, my friends, is the greatest lesson of all.

~

"Sir? Coffee or tea?" It takes me a second to realize the flight attendant is talking to me. I look up from my laptop. "Tea, please," I answer as she deftly manoeuvres the silver teapot into a pouring position. I slide up the window shade and gaze down at the jagged peaks below. What a formidable obstacle those mountains must have been to those first Canadian explorers, I think to myself. And today we just fly right over them—in a little more than an hour. It always amazes me how dedicated those voyageurs must have been. They had no idea what they were in for when they started out. But they persevered, despite incredible challenges.

This gets me thinking. I'm not sure I would have started writing this book back in 2010 had I known how much work it would eventually turn out to be. Juggling writing and a full-time financial planning practice has perhaps been my biggest challenge. Just ask my esteemed associate, Jonah Angeles, who has "held the fort" many times for me while I've been off on a sojourn trying to complete this project. But now that I'm near the end, I wouldn't trade the experience, joy and satisfaction I've felt doing it for anything else in the world. After all, how many writers get an opportunity to tell a story like this—especially one about their father?

I turn back towards the flight attendant, watching as she reaches across the passenger sitting next to me, carefully extending the little plastic tray with my tea on it. I take the cup from the tray and smile in thanks. She smiles in response and moves on to the next row. Then I look down and realize that I have nowhere to put my tea, because my laptop and my notes are taking up all the space.

The man in the next seat turns towards me. "Do you want to put that down on my tray until you put your computer away?" he offers. "Would be a shame to spill it. Here, put it on my tray while you organize your stuff." I smile in gratitude. "Thanks," I reply. I carefully place the cup on his tray and then close the lid of my laptop.

"Excuse me for asking," he says, "but are you a writer? I couldn't help but see your notes. Looks to me like you're working on some sort of a biography?"

I grin. "Well, actually, I'm a financial advisor. And the book's about my dad." The man raises his eyebrows. He's probably a few years older than I am. He's wearing a suit—a nice one. A sharp dresser. I glance down, feeling underdressed in my jeans and comfy fleece sweat top, ideal for travelling but not exactly "Dress for success" attire. I'd run out of clean clothes yesterday at Dad's place, and we were so busy I didn't get around to throwing a load into the washer.

I slide my laptop into its case and move the cup onto my own tray. "My dad's a Prairie boy who grew up during the Great Depression," I explain. "He's always been a curious guy, so when he was in his late fifties, he had a few investment ideas he wanted to try out in the stock market." I can't tell if the man is really interested or if this is just one of those plane conversations that doesn't go anywhere, but I keep talking anyway. "His thing was leveraging. He was a long-term kind of guy who bought quality and ended up developing an investment program that's done quite well over the years."

The man nods his head slowly. "Well, what do you know? You say he was a Prairie boy? Where from? I'm from Saskatchewan myself. It's always good to hear about someone from 'back home' doing well for themselves."

I laugh. "He was born in a little place called Wakaw," I say, confident that his next question will be: Where the heck is that? Instead he replies: "Well, I've never actually been there—but my dad grew up on a farm near Prince Albert, so we used to stop for gas and a treat at the south end of town on the way home. Me, I was born just outside of Saskatoon. Back in those days, just outside of Saskatoon was just that, if you know what I mean. Not like today where everything is suburbs, swallowed up by the city. Back then you could actually see the stars at night. That's all changed, but stargazing is one of my favourite memories of growing up on the Prairies."

"So," I inquire, "you still live in Saskatoon?" He laughs. "Nah, I live in Calgary now. Been out this way for about ten years now. All that oil money drew me out and I ended up staying. That's where all the action has been—until recently, that is. Now things are booming back home. You know, potash, uranium and all that new-found oil wealth. Saskatchewan's really heating up. The farmers aren't exactly hurting either. Now, if we can only keep the Roughriders going, we'll have everything just the way we want it," he adds, laughing.

"Think you'll retire in Calgary?" I ask. "Hell, no," he retorts. "I want to retire out somewhere small, where I can have a little land of my own. There's something about connecting with the land that's never left me. Got to have it. You know, a garden, sit on the back porch, watch the day go by. That type of thing. Maybe dabble in the market a bit, who knows?"

My seatmate pauses for a few seconds, then changes the subject: "So, what's the pitch? You've got your dad's story. How're you going to sell it? What's the hook?"

I grimace and take a deep breath in. "Well, that's just it. There's so much to tell . . ." He cuts me off. "Ahh. Clearly you're an advisor, not a writer. Got a ton to say, so you try to say it all. I know the type." He clears his throat.

"Listen," he says, "I've read a ton of financial books. Most of them don't get the job done, really. Bombarded me with everything there was to tell, which means I don't get much out of any of them. Sounds like you've got something really unique here. A real-life example of a small-town guy who's done well. That's a rare commodity, especially these days, you know, with all the problems in the market over the last few years." I nod, acknowledging his point.

"The way I look at it," he says, "you've just got to show people what your dad did. They'll figure out whether or not it's right for them. Sure, tell them what worked and what didn't. But the key, as Tom Cruise famously said, is to 'Show me the money!' Right?" His replication of Cruise's voice is nowhere close to accurate. Still, I smile in appreciation of his effort.

I look down. My tea has stopped steaming. We're probably due to land soon. I take a quick sip of tea, now lukewarm, then launch in. "Okay, here it is, plain and simple. If my dad wouldn't have leveraged, wouldn't have taken any risks, just bought bonds like many people his age were advised to do, he'd be sitting on about $32,000 a year retirement income from his investments. As it is, even with the market downturn a few years back, he's still sitting on income of $300,000 a year, when all is said and done."

My new friend nods slowly. "That's impressive," he says. "So what's the take-away for the reader? Are they going to read it and think, 'That's one lucky so-and-so,' or are they going to read it and think, 'Hey, maybe I can do that too'? Because that, my friend, is ultimately what matters—if you're trying to sell books, that is."

The seatbelt sign lights up, eliciting a few clicks, and a flight attendant starts the landing announcements. I shift in my seat, waiting for what seems like an eternity for the in-flight directions to finish, then jump back in. "Actually, the things that made my dad his money don't have much to do with his financial ability. They've got more to do with his outlook on life. You know, work hard, don't live beyond your means, be patient, invest for the long haul, that kind of thing. Sure, the financial know-how was important, but knowledge alone doesn't help if you don't plan for the future."

My colleague smiles. "Once a Prairie boy . . . , eh? Bet he still buys half-price pies, too, just like all those old guys," he says. "My dad's the same. Nearly ninety years old, and I can't get him to spring for a shirt that doesn't come from the supermarket. He takes one look at me when I visit and launches into 'How much did that suit cost, son?' and so on. Drives me crazy—but at the end of the day, he's right."

I feel the plane tucking into a turn, and I realize we're probably over Vancouver by now. I glance out the window and see the deep-blue hue of the ocean sparkling up against snow-covered shorelines. Far beyond I see a city swathed in white and wonder how the good people of Vancouver are handling the snow.

The man leans over and looks out my window. "Wow," he exclaims. "Look at those mountains, how they meet the ocean! Even with all the snow out there, this still looks like a great place to live." Then, in the same breath, he mutters: "Bet it's expensive as hell, eh?"

Then, returning to our previous discussion, he says: "Sounds like what made your dad successful are those things he learned when he was growing up. By the time we've grown up, our personalities are pretty much set. And that guides us for the rest of our lives, don't you think?" I nod. To be honest, I think he's oversimplifying things a little, but it looks like we'll be landing any minute, so instead I just reply: "The way I see it, it was my dad's strength of character and his outlook on life that brought him his success. It's also what got him through when times got tough."

"And times have been tough, lately," the man adds, solemnly. I feel the vibration of the landing gear extending. "Yes, they have been," I reply. "But even when times did get tough, Dad's motto was always to be patient, keep getting stuff done, and hope that next year would be better."

"Ha!" the man replies. "I can almost hear my dad saying the same thing. Those old guys are the real deal. Like they never left the farm," he says. He reaches into the left breast pocket of his suit jacket and fishes out a shiny business card. He extends his hand as he gives it to me, saying, "Hey, my name is Dave Roberts. What a pleasure to meet you and hear all about your dad's story."

"Likewise, Dave. My name is Doug Hodgins," I reply, as I shake his hand.

Dave carries right on. "Hey, I'd love to read that book once it's finished. When you've got it printed, give me a call. I'll take a few off your hands. I know someone who would get a real kick out of reading it." I glance down at his card, mentally noting his name before carefully tucking it into my wallet. "It would make a nice birthday present for the old man," he says, "reading about a Saskatchewan guy, a lot like himself, who did well. Anyway, keep me posted on your progress."

There's a bump as the wheels touch down on the runway. The engines roar as the plane slows down. Home sweet home. The plane taxis to the gate. The seatbelt sign switches off and people start getting up. Must be a Pavlovian response, I think to myself, this need to stand up and try to get off before everyone else, even though we all recognize the futility of the quest. I just sit in my seat, waiting. There's no sense in trying to squeeze ahead.

My seatmate Dave stands up. He reaches into the overhead bin to grab his suitbag. Then his face drops down to meet mine. "Do you ever worry," he says, "that when you leave your dad, it might be the last time you ever see him?" His eyes narrow. "I mean, I always wonder about that myself, with my father. What if the last time really was the *last time,* you know? I tell you, Doug, I make sure that I savour all the moments I get with him, you know—all the little things he does, his mannerisms, hell, even his quirks—because hey, you never know. Nobody knows what tomorrow will bring."

I don't know how to respond at first, so I just nod slowly. "I do think about it," I reply. "But maybe I just haven't come to terms with it, really. I just hope I can finish this book before, you know . . ."

Dave smiles. "Sounds like your dad is the type of guy who wouldn't shuffle off this mortal coil until his work here is done. I'll bet even if he was going to die, he'd be too stubborn to let go until he was good and ready!" He laughs, which evokes a nervous chuckle from me as well. "Don't worry, Doug, I'm sure your dad's going to be around for a while yet. Probably can't wait to see the look on some of his old buddies' faces when he shows them the book. That would make any man proud.

"What you're doing for your dad, writing this book, that's a great thing. The way I see it, it's one of the best things a son could do for his father."

The line starts moving, single file, towards the front of the plane. I pull out the in-flight magazine, flipping through it while I wait. Dave picks up his carry-on luggage and says, "Good luck with the book." I look over to thank him, but he's already moved down the aisle. I stay seated a moment longer. Then I stand up, tuck my laptop case under my arm, and join the other passengers slowly exiting the plane.

~

The first thing I notice is the snow. It's too early in the season for this to happen in Vancouver, I think to myself. Apparently, there has been an unexpected cold snap and an overnight dump of snow along with it—if you call three inches of snow a dump. This should be interesting.

What we from the Prairies take for granted is perceived as a state of emergency in Vancouver. Traffic is essentially at a standstill as summer tires spin out of control on the icy streets that now resemble one big skating rink. I overhear another passenger say that the authorities have put out a weather advisory urging Vancouverites to stay off city streets unless absolutely necessary to travel. School officials have sent children home early today and issued closure notices for tomorrow due to the extreme conditions—too dangerous for children to be out in $-8°$ weather— and this in addition to the snow, for heaven's sake!

I chuckle to myself as I step onto the moving walkway. My thoughts drift back to Dad. He's probably sitting at his kitchen table back in Lethbridge, gazing out at the gently falling snowflakes, smiling to himself about our west coast city grinding to a halt. I'm not sure why, maybe it's the emotion of a son writing about his father or the fact that I've thoroughly enjoyed this special time together, but I can't stop wondering: what's going to happen when Dad's gone?

The words expressed by my seatmate Dave on the plane haunt me. What if this really was the last time I got to see Dad? What then? No more early-morning phone conversations swapping investment stories. No more bantering back and forth about the state of the economy. No more fatherly advice.

One day—could be any day now—his life and story will be a thing of the past, and we'll take over, just like all sons and daughters have done through the ages.

These thoughts are racing through my mind as I step from the moving walkway back onto the carpet—its swirling patterns mirroring what's going on in my head as I make my way through Canada's second-busiest airport. I approach the luggage carousel and catch a glimpse of my suitcase moving along its brushed aluminum surface. I wait for a moment until it arrives, hoist it off, snap the handle out and head for the exit. As the doors slide open, a blast of cold air awakens my senses and I step out into a world of snow and ice. Am I really in Vancouver? A different set of airport sights and sounds permeates my senses—people shuffling, horns honking, a lone traffic warden directing traffic. It's chaos out here, a real free-for-all. I don't know why, but for some reason the guy organizing the taxi line has vacated his post, so it's absolute bedlam as people try to flag down a cab. I move towards the curb, extending my arm to catch a passing cabby's attention. No luck.

The wintry scene takes me back to winters on the Prairies. I think of another time and place: January 12, 1978, Claresholm, Alberta. My mind turns back to my dad. I imagine him sitting in his parked car outside the bank, engine idling to keep him warm while he waited. One last look at his papers to make sure everything was in good order. What was he thinking? Was he apprehensive about going in? Sure, the numbers made good sense to him—but would the banker see it the same way?

I can see him glancing up from his notes, watching the clerk flip over the OPEN FOR BUSINESS sign at precisely 9:00 a.m. Taking a deep breath to compose himself, he opened the door and stepped into the cold air. He was wearing his best suit and overcoat, his hair neatly trimmed and combed to the side. Dad always said a man's shoes were the best indicator of how well he dressed, so he was looking sharp in his perfectly polished black dress shoes. Dad's footsteps crunched on the snow-covered sidewalk as he made his way into the bank. He walked with purpose—this was a business meeting, after all.

Another cab flies by without stopping. I notice the chill in the air but I'm struck by a somewhat surreal feeling—almost like I'm right there with Dad walking into that bank. Then it hits me . . . I'm already past the age that Dad was at the time he began his investment journey. It's the first time I've thought about this in the three years since I began this project. I've been so focused on the story that I hadn't really taken the time to ponder the significance of this.

Another gust of frigid air hits my face. Back to reality. It's bloody cold out here without a decent jacket! A taxi pulls towards the curb, but it cruises past me to a man wearing an elegant long black coat. Seems like the mantra "Dress for success" also applies to hailing a cab. Stay positive. I blow into my hands to ward off the chill. Next one's mine.

Just then a taxi swerves right in front of me, the driver popping out like he's spring-loaded. "Where to?" he asks as he opens the trunk and lifts my suitcase inside. "Home," I say, and I give him my address as we climb in. The driver says: "Damn, that's some cold, eh?" I laugh. "Sure is," I reply.

As we pull out I realize I need to make a stop on the way home. I grab my phone and dial a familiar number. After a few rings, a pleasant female voice answers. "How may I direct your call?"

"Bob Newman in loans," I reply.

"One moment, please," the voice responds as she puts me on hold and I hear the familiar sound of elevator music. I glance out the cab window, watching a plane land gracefully as we pick up speed and head for the bridge. The music cuts out and I hear: "Bob Newman speaking." I take a deep breath.

"Bob," I say, "it's Doug Hodgins. Any chance you have an opening today?" Silence. I have a brief moment of doubt. What if it isn't the right time? What if he can't fit me in today? Then the reply: "Sure, Doug, I've got a 3:30 slot available."

"Perfect," I reply. "I'm on the way. Let's get the paperwork done on that investment loan I've been talking about but never seem to get around to setting up."

Outside the cab, the cityscape becomes a blur. Houses, trees, cars and people blend into a single image. I'm not really looking as I have other thoughts on my mind. I hear my dad's voice once again. *Strip it all back, Douglas, so you can see the stars. That's the only way to see what's really important.*

Got it, Dad. Everything we've talked about all these years finally makes sense. I just needed to slow down, listen more carefully and hear the message. We both know that his time as an investor is winding down and mine is just beginning. It's time to pass the torch—time for the student to become the teacher.

Take it, Douglas, the story's all yours. It's your turn. It's not perfect but I think it's a pretty good start. Run with it, make it better . . . then pass it on . . .

Don't worry, Dad. It's in good hands.

Acknowledgements

ANYONE WHO HAS EVER WRITTEN A BOOK KNOWS THAT IT WOULDN'T HAVE HAPPENED WITHOUT A LOT OF SUPPORT ALONG THE WAY. I've received more than I could ever have dreamed possible.

First I want to thank my parents, Rankin and my late mother, Daphne, who somehow convinced me I could accomplish anything I wanted if I believed in myself and backed up that belief with a lot of goal-oriented hard work. Whatever self-discipline I have was passed on by my father, while my creative side came from my mother. I couldn't have asked for better role models. In short, I lucked out in the parent "lottery."

I've received tremendous support for this project from my siblings, Bill, Robert, Valerie and John. I want to extend a special thanks to John, who worked alongside me from about 2003 to 2007 in researching and developing investment and tax planning strategies based on Dad's program. This eventually gave me the impetus to get all our ideas down on paper and start writing in 2007. The market retrenchment of 2008–09 put everything on hold until 2010.

A chance business conversation with MRS Trust executives Paul Stadnick and Mario Rossi in May 2010 at Gotham Steakhouse in Vancouver convinced me I had a story that needed to be told. It's amazing how an evening of friendship, fine dining and a few libations can open one's mind. Anyway, this is where the seed for the book was replanted. Thanks, guys, for a great idea and a fabulous evening.

I've received ongoing support and encouragement from many colleagues in the financial services industry. Todd Haibeck, Jason Kean, David Kendall, Rahim Mulji, Marcus Slade, Chris Toomey and Jim Tsiakos have all taken a keen interest in my project, often inspiring me to carry on when my spirits were at a low point. Marcus also introduced me to Larry Distillio from Mackenzie Financial, who guided me as my "project coach" through the past three years. Thanks for the mantra "Progress, not perfection," Larry. I've leaned on Larry and that adage many times over the course of writing this book.

I'm fortunate to work with an extremely talented group of colleagues at Assante Vancouver Centre. Thanks for all your ideas, interest and patience along the way. Special thanks to Paul Lermitte and Jonah Angeles. Paul has been a trailblazer to me with practical advice that only a published author can give, while Jonah supported both me and my clients on a daily basis throughout this epic journey. Thanks as well to my clients, who have encouraged me from day one to keep the dream alive and get this thing done.

I wouldn't have had the opportunity to write a book or been successful in business if I hadn't chosen two excellent partners, Doug Leard and Don Proteau, to open the Hodgins, Leard & Proteau branch of FPC Investments back in 1987. Not only are these two gentlemen among the best planners around, their business acumen carried our firm from inception. Doug and Don are like family to me, and I'm very proud of how far we and the rest of our partners have come from our humble beginnings.

I've had a loyal group of friends whom I've called upon to help me with everything from proofreading to writing to just bouncing ideas around. This list includes Grant Block, David Enns, Chad Friesen, Erik Gustafson, cousin Grant Hodgins,

Mike Longhi, Dale Rondeau, Ray and Shirley Spaxman, and Sue Wastie. Thanks to each of you for your special contributions.

The team I assembled to work with me on the various phases of book production is as good as it gets.

Josh Hergesheimer, my writer, and I spent countless hours over two years fleshing out this story. Thanks to Josh for his insight, creativity and ability to pull off "all-nighters" when anything less would not have been good enough. I marvel at what we've created, Josh.

My son, Dan Hodgins, has been like a beacon to me, someone I could turn to whenever I needed advice or a second opinion on any part of the process. Dan's input now ramps up as we switch into marketing mode. His expertise in communication is just what's needed to get this story into the hands of the reading public. I'm thrilled to have you on my team, Dan!

Naomi Pauls of Paper Trail Publishing has been a dream editor to work with. I think I'm what you would call a "project," but she's been a true professional in guiding me with clarity, focus and class, even making me look like a writer along the way. Thanks, Naomi—to quote Tina Turner, "You're simply the best."

Last in the production line but first on my list of fabulous book designers is Nathan Waddington, who's taken an average manuscript and made it into a thing of beauty. Our creative collaboration in fine-tuning the design of this book has been an immensely rewarding experience. Nathan also introduced me to Yvonne Ren, illustrator extraordinaire, who helped us zero in on a front cover concept that conveyed exactly what we were looking for. What a pleasure to work with you both, Nathan and Yvonne.

If you ever decide to do anything that involves the written word, make me the first call because these are the people you need to work with to make a good book great.

Thanks to my daughter, Amy, for her love and support. I'm super proud of you and everything you do.

Lastly, I want to thank my partner in life, Kelly Isaura Souza da Conceicao. I met Kelly in Rio de Janeiro in June 2010 about the time I started writing this book. Over the next two years I made numerous trips to Rio as it turned out to be a perfect place for writing. My routine there was always the same—start my morning with a run on Copacabana beach and spend the rest of the day writing while Kelly was at work. Talk about fabulous working conditions. A year ago Kelly and her daughter Marcela decided to move to Vancouver so we could start a new life together. I couldn't be happier. *Obrigado para você, amor da minha vida !*

About the Author

DOUG HODGINS GREW UP IN THE NORTHEASTERN SASKATCHEWAN TOWN OF TISDALE, where he learned small-town Prairie values such as loyalty, hard work and the importance of community that still serve him well in Vancouver, where he has lived since 1981.

Doug graduated from the University of Saskatchewan with a degree in commerce in 1976 and the University of Lethbridge with a bachelor of arts in physical education in 1980. He joined the financial planning profession in 1982 and holds Certified Financial Planner and Registered Financial Planner designations.

Doug joined partners Doug Leard and Don Proteau to open Hodgins, Leard, Proteau & Associates Ltd., a branch of FPC Investments, in downtown Vancouver's Scotia Tower in 1987. Twenty-six years later, he still practises with his original partners (and nine others!) at Scotia Tower in what has evolved into the Assante Vancouver Centre branch with client assets under management of more than $1 billion.

Doug's main focus is to help clients develop and implement risk-appropriate investment, tax and financial planning strategies to reach their most important life goals. With the publication of *Millionaire Down the Road*, Doug is looking forward to using lessons learned from his dad to show clients and readers how critically important tax-efficient investing is in retirement wealth accumulation.

Index

A & E Pierce Corporation, 23
Alberta tax rates, 94, 98, 104, 151
Angeles, Jonah, 174
attitude. *See* investment outlook

Baird, Larry, 41
bank loan
    initial, 1, 2, 105, 182–83
    for investment, 83, 133
    repayment, 140, 144, 145
Bank of Montreal (BMO), 151
Bank of Nova Scotia (BNS), 120, 151
banks, 2, 111, 120, 133, 150
bank stocks
    capital gains analysis (Fig. 12), 151
    focus on, 79, 80, 88, 112, 115
    returns, TD bank, 56–57
    as safe investment, 111, 129–30, 145
book project, 43, 58, 106, 107, 159–61,
    174–75. *See also* pitching the
    book
British Columbia tax rates, 70, 71, 94
buy-and-hold strategy, 76, 87, 88, 95,
    134, 170

Canada Revenue Agency (CRA), 69,
    70, 71, 91
capital, sources of, 2, 132–34,
    135 (Fig. 7)

capital gains, 95, 103, 134.
    See also returns
capital retention
    and buy-and-hold strategy, 130–31
    as investment goal, 55
    tax deferral and, 93, 95, 103, 134
    and wealth creation, 166, 169
Carr, Jimmy, 38
cash flow management, 84, 144–45,
    148–50, 149 (Fig. 11), 153
CIBC, 2, 120, 133, 151
compound interest, 54–56, 59, 68,
    76, 169
consumer spending, 46–49, 51,
    98–99
Continental Life Insurance
    Company, 38
Corba, Kenneth, xiii–xiv, 8, 50–51
credit, 46–47, 49, 166

"death and taxes," 91, 93, 152
debt, good *vs.* bad, 166
debt management, 137–40, 144
debt outstanding, 124–25 (Fig. 1),
    126 (Fig. 2), 140 (Fig. 8)
dividend income, 26, 70, 103, 144–45,
    148. *See also* returns
dividend payouts, 76, 111, 129, 145, 150
dollar cost averaging, 113, 135, 137

economy, 20, 49
   Depression-era, 22–23, 25, 48
   and interest rates, 83–84, 145
   and stock markets, 10, 76, 118, 167
Einstein, Albert (quoted), 54
emotions, managing, 3–4, 49, 82–
   83, 137

farming
   compared to investing, 3, 108, 109,
      170, 173
   Depression-era, 22–23
   and long-term thinking, 25,
      171–72
financial advisors, 16, 45, 55, 68–69,
   83
foreign investments, 79–80

gains. See capital gains; returns
GIC investment, 56, 59
gifts to family, 47, 66, 113, 117, 165
Gilbertson, Virgil, 31
granary story, 27, 28, 29–32, 85, 161
Great Depression
   economics of, 22, 48
   impact of, 3, 4, 23–26
   lessons of, 92, 170, 173–74
   surviving the, 119, 120

Hill, Bob, 40
Hodgins, Daphne (née Dundas), 2,
   38, 50–51, 132, 172
Hodgins, Douglas
   early life, 1, 38–39, 162
   education, 35, 41
   as financial advisor, 16, 45, 55, 83
   first mortgage, 86
   Prairie roots, 21, 29, 39–40, 44

Hodgins, John, 8, 13, 39, 45, 83, 112,
   136
Hodgins, Kenneth Wallace, 12,
   20–21, 23, 30, 81–82
Hodgins, Rachel (née Rankin), 19,
   25, 28
Hodgins, Robert, 38, 41
Hodgins, Valerie (Lowen), 39, 42
Hodgins, Wilfred (Rankin's father),
   20, 22, 23, 25, 28–30, 38
Hodgins, Wilfred <u>Rankin</u>
   character, 42, 53–54, 171
   early life, 19–24, 88, 162
   early life lessons, 3, 26, 170,
      173–74
   education and career, 21, 28–34,
      38–42, 85
   life values (see values)
   marriage and children, 38–39
   retirement, 41–42, 108–9, 110,
      135, 144
   views: on big-city money guys, 51,
      128–29, 139, 167; on the book,
      17, 18, 44, 61–62, 123, 162–63;
      on government, 46, 48, 92, 104
Hodgins, William ("Bill"), 38, 41, 42
Hodgins, William ("Bill") Arnold,
   23, 28, 31
home ownership, 86–87, 118, 166

income taxes, 149 (Fig. 11), 152–53.
   See also taxation
income tax planning
   need for, 91
   for retirement, 70–71, 103–4
   strategies, 69–71, 99–102
   See also tax deferral; tax
      reduction strategies

interest, compound, 54–56, 59, 68
interest expense
    matching strategy, 142, 144–45,
      148
    as tax deductible, 67, 71, 80, 84
interest rates, 6, 83–84, 108, 141–42,
    144, 145
investing
    compared to farming, 3, 108, 170,
      173
    compared to sports, 109
"invest it and forget it," 172–73
investment capital, 2, 132–34,
    135 (Fig. 7)
investment history
    1980s, 108–9, 110–11
    1990s, 112–13
    2000 to 2012, 117–21
    entry years, 107–8
    summary, xiii, 26, 124–25 (Fig. 1)
    and tech stock boom, 114–15
    track record, 15–16, 65–66
investment outlook
    focus on principles, 4, 131–32, 169
    patience / persistence, 3, 24–25,
      171, 174
    respect for markets, 10
    See also long-term outlook;
      values
investment portfolio
    diversification, 80
    graphic summary, 126 (Fig. 2)
    management, 73–74, 76, 128–32
    and risk, 69, 78–79
    See also losses; returns
investment strategy
    choosing solid companies, 26, 65,
      76, 95

and consistency, 121, 137, 169, 173
and financial advisors, 68–69
getting an edge, 9, 55, 74
getting it right, 109
and personality, 128, 131, 167–68
Rankin's, 108, 113, 117
See also buy-and-hold strategy;
    investment outlook; tax
    reduction strategies
investor personality, 68, 128–29, 131,
    167–68

Johnson, Bill, 38

Kilden, Ole, 28

leveraged investing
    about, 63–66, 76
    entry into, 105, 107–8, 169
    examples of, 66–68
    as long-term strategy, 128
    mortgage as a form of, 86
    not for everyone, viii, 46, 73
    understanding, 168
    See also losses; returns; risks of
      leveraged investing; tax savings
lifestyle, 47, 98–99, 166
life values. See values
long-term outlook
    farming and, 25, 170, 171–72
    investment and, 26, 57, 88, 128–29
    and market volatility, 83
    and reinvesting tax savings, 133
    and tech stock boom, 114, 116
losses
    amplification of, 88–89
    history of, 10, 11, 110, 112, 118, 143
    in international funds, 79–80

Lowen, Mike, 42
Lowen, Valerie (née Hodgins), 39, 42

margin calls, 10, 84, 88
margin ratio(s)
    average, 141 (Fig. 9)
    management, 63, 138–39, 141–45
    summary, 124–25 (Fig. 1),
        143 (Fig. 10), 156 (Fig. 13)
    and unrealized gains, 134
margin risk, 84–85
matching strategy
    income to interest expense, 142,
        144–45, 148
    own money with bank money,
        84, 138
mathematical knowledge, 2, 34
Molstad, Alfred, 23, 119
mortgages, 86–87, 118
mutual funds, 11–12, 79–80, 109

Northern Light High School, 28, 32

pension income, 69, 70, 94, 98, 153,
    171
philosophy. *See* investment outlook
Pimco Equity Advisors, xiv, 8
pitching the book, 17–18, 176, 177–78

real estate, 86–88, 107–8
recession of 1981–82, 108
retirement, 50, 70–71, 103–4, 152–53
returns
    amplification of, 76, 88–89
    on bank stocks (Fig. 12), 151
    "best year ever" (2009), 120, 144
    compound: five-year, 130 (Fig. 5),
        156 (Fig. 13); ten-year, 131 (Fig. 6)

with compound interest, 54–55,
    56, 59
history of, 111, 113, 117, 121, 136, 138
margin ratio and, 141–42
net investment, 127 (Fig. 3)
one-year, 124–25 (Fig. 1),
    129 (Fig. 4)
summary, 155–56, 165, 169, 172
and taxation, 66–68, 70, 71
variability and, 79, 127–28
See also capital gains; dividend
    income
risks, investment, 73–74, 76, 77–81,
    167–68
risks of leveraged investing
    amplification of gains / losses, 63,
        76, 78, 88–89, 168
    amplification of risk, 77
    summary, 82–85
    things can go wrong, 45–46
Royal Bank, 112, 120
Royal Trust bankruptcy, 111–12
RRIF income, 69, 100, 103, 153, 171
RRSPS, 69, 100, 101–3, 104, 153

saving money, 46–47, 49–50, 87,
    165–66
saving taxes. *See* tax savings
Scotiabank, 120, 151
short-term thinking, 88, 116, 171
short-term trading, 68, 144, 167
spending, consumer, 46–49, 51,
    98–99
starting to invest, 53–54, 58
stock market
    risk, 77–78
    short-term volatility, 83, 170
    variability, 10, 68, 82, 167, 168

stock market corrections
about, 3, 76, 82, 83, 133
of 1987, 4, 10, 110, 136, 138
of 2001, 4, 117
of 2008–09, 7–10, 12–13, 85, 118–20, 137, 139, 142
stock purchases, 110–11, 120, 144, 145, 149
stock purchasing patterns, 113, 135–37
stock sales, 88, 120, 137, 142–43, 148, 150–51
Struthers, Ike, 39
subprime mortgage crisis, 118

taxation, 80–81, 98, 142.
See also income taxes
tax deferral
and buy-and-hold strategy, 76, 117
and capital retention, 93, 95, 134
importance of, 70
strategy, 102–4, 150–52, 151
tax reduction strategies
about, 68, 69–71, 101–2
deferring tax (see tax deferral)
"four kinds of dollars," 94–95
overview, 147, 170–71
reducing current taxes, 148–50
for retirement, 70–71, 103–4, 152–53

tax savings
about, 94–96
comparisons, 152–53, 171
as investment capital, 133–34
leveraging and, 65, 67, 71, 73, 76
TD Bank, 56–57
tech stock boom, 113–16
Templeton funds, 11–12, 79, 111, 112
Tisdale, Saskatchewan, 39, 40
Trimark funds, 11, 79, 112

University of Saskatchewan, 34, 41
unrealized capital gains, 95, 103, 134

values, 4, 24–25
community, 12, 40
discipline, 57, 116, 131
education, 28, 35, 37
frugality, 85, 98, 166
gratitude, 23, 45
patience, 21, 26, 174, 179
persistence, 3, 119, 173

wealth creation, 54, 68, 69, 73, 169
World War I, 20
World War II, 34